Copyright © 2013 by Karima Sperling
All rights reserved. This book or any portion thereof may not be reproduced or used in any manner whatsoever without the express written permission of the publisher except for the use of brief quotations in a book review.

Printed in the United States of America

First Edition Standard Color, 2013

ISBN 978-0-9913003-0-3

Little Bird Books
littlebirdbooksink@gmail.com

STANDARD EDITION

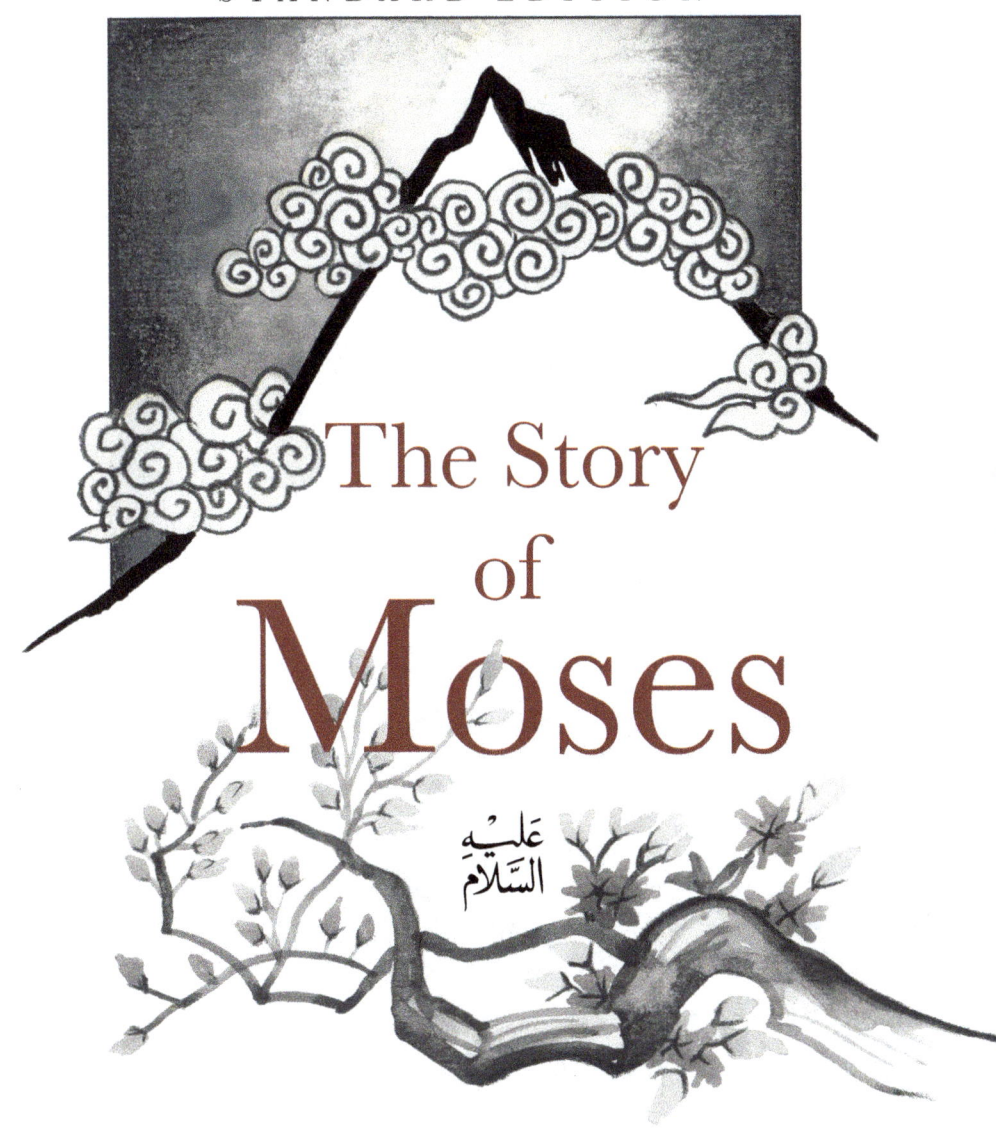

The Story of Moses
عَلَيْهِ السَّلَام

Karima Sperling

Design by Nabil Ibrahim

Bismillah ar-Rahman ar-Rahim

We begin in the Name of the One to whom all thanks are due: Allah, Cherisher of the worlds and Creator of all the stories. We send our love and respect to His Beloved, Muhammad Mustafa ﷺ, by whose light the world and its stories continue to be illuminated.

We send our love and respect to all the 124,000 prophets who have carried their Lord's message in all times and in all lands. We hope that this book in some small way opens the hearts of the readers to the nature of our shared journey. Only by knowing our selves and our relationship to the One who created us, can there be the possibility of truly loving and respecting each other.

Table of Contents

Preface.. 10

Symbols Used In This Book............................... 13

Dedication.. 14

Acknowledgments... 16

1. Introduction... 18
2. A Prophet Comes To Egypt........................ 26
3. The Rooster Of The Throne....................... 34
4. The Fruit Of The Tree................................. 40
5. Dreams... 46
6. A Star Is Born... 52
7. Lost... 58
8. Found.. 64
9. Returned.. 70
10. Names... 76
11. Pharaoh's Beard... 82
12. Growing Up In Two Worlds....................... 88
13. A Life For A Life... 96
14. A Stranger... 102

15. Shuayb ﷺ	108
16. A Shepherd's Staff	116
17. The Fire That Did Not Burn	124
18. The Hand And The Staff	132
19. The Mission And The Message	140
20. Return To Egypt	148
21. Delivering The Message	154
22. A Sign For Pharaoh	162
23. Dragon Magic	170
24. A House In Paradise	176
25. For Whom The River Stops	184
26. Nine Warning Signs	190
27. A Community Of Believers	198
28. Buried Treasure	206
29. Towering Arrogance	214
30. Finding Yusuf ﷺ	**222**
31. The Ninth Sign	228
32. An Opening In The Sea	234
33. The Other Side	242

34. Forbidden Gold	250
35. The Heights	258
36. Righteous Anger	268
37. Hearts Of Gold	278
38. Tablets And Tawrah	286
39. Tabut And Tabernacle	294
40. A Giant Mistake	302
41. Bewildered	310
42. The Sign Of The Fish	318
43. The Beak Of The Bird	324
44. The Tail Of The Cow	332
45. Attributes Of The Prophets	340
46. A Marvelous Tree	348
47. An Angel's Eye	356
48. Conclusion	366
Glossary	374
Bibliography	378
About The Author	380
About The Artist	381

Mawlana Shaykh Muhammad Nazim Adil Al-Haqqani

Preface

This book was written at the explicit request of Mawlana Shaykh Muhammad Nazim Adil Al-Haqqani, our beloved master and the Grandshaykh of the Exalted Naqshbandi Tariqah, and we dedicate it to him. For almost a century he has dedicated himself to serving his Master, Sayyidina Muhammad ﷺ, and his Lord by guiding with unfailing love and attention all those who have had the good fortune to come under his eye. He has never faltered or rested in setting a perfect example of the right way or urgently warning against the wrong way. By walking firmly in the footsteps of the Prophet ﷺ he has illuminated that path for all of us. He remains the only trustworthy standard we know by which to measure the confusing world around us. Through him the words of the Prophet ﷺ and the Words of the Lord become accessible and real. These are his words:

"Nowadays people have no mind. There are books about the life of the Prophet ﷺ for scholars and there are books for the common people. Don't teach the common people what is meant for the scholars. Don't teach law, jurisprudence, or

doctrine. Leave this. We should be concerned instead with the things that make people connect to the heart of the Beloved, the Prophet Muhammad ﷺ, with love and praise, with respect and appreciation. This is what is important.

"'So relate the stories that perhaps they may reflect.' (7:176)

"The Quran doesn't order us to teach law, or doctrine, but it does order us to tell the stories. Tell the stories from the Quran, the Hadith, about the prophets, their companions and the saints. It is not our responsibility to verify the details, only to relate the stories. People may think on them and take something. Don't worry if the stories actually happened, where or how. Just remind the people so that they may reflect and so that their hearts may incline towards the hereafter.

"Tell the stories: they will have an effect. This is what is important."

(From a talk given on September 10, 2011 by Mawlana Shaykh Nazim al Haqqani, in Lefke Cyprus.)

May this book serve to accomplish his intention.
Wa min Allah at-tawfiq: From God comes the Enabling Grace.

Symbols Used In This Book

ﷺ – Salla Allahu alayhi wa s-sallam. This is the prayer that is said whenever the name of the Prophet Muhammad ﷺ is mentioned, asking Allah to send him peace and blessings.

؏ – Alayhi s-salam. This is the prayer that is said whenever the names of any of the prophets are mentioned, meaning peace be upon him.

ؓ ؓ – Radhia Allahu anhu, radhia Allahu anha. This is said in the memory of saints and companions of the prophets, meaning may the Pleasure of Allah be upon him or her.

Quotations from The Quran are offset from the text by a double space and are followed with a paranthesis in which the first number refers to the chapter and the second number to the verse being quoted.

Mawlana Shaykh Nazim and Hajja Aminah Adil

Dedication

This book is dedicated to Hajja Aminah Adil, the late wife of Mawlana Shaykh Muhammad Nazim Adil Al-Haqqani. Throughout her life she told the stories of the prophets and saints, first to her own children, and then to us, her spiritual children. She told the stories in her own inimitable style, in the way they should be told. She loved the stories and her love gave them life. She lived the stories as an example for all of us to see. There is no way to relate one of the stories and not remember, miss, and be thankful for this remarkable woman, Hajja Anne, our Mother. We hope that our humble effort would please her.

Acknowledgments

Karima would like to thank Nabil for his amazing artistry and to acknowledge the much valued contributions of – Munir Sperling for support on all levels; Aminah Sperling Alptekin who formatted the book and is a computer wizard; Alia Sperling Nazeer for proofreading and editing; Sanaa Makhlouf and Abdul Jalil Stelzer for reading and commentary; Radhia Miller for her always honest opinion; Salim and Hagar Spohr for their expertise and advice; H. Bahauddin Adil for pushing; Haniya, Humayra, Hamza, Layka, Ibrahim, Ishaq, and Ghalib, for loving stories and giving hope.

Nabil would like to offer his heartfelt gratitude to Mawlana Shaykh Nazim for showing him the creative gifts hidden within himself and Karima for providing, in a time of difficulty, the means of their expression.

1.

Introduction

"All that We relate to you of the stories of the prophets is in order that We may make firm your heart. And in them there comes to you the Truth, as well as an encouragement and a reminder for the believers." (11:120)

The aim of this book is to reintroduce the reader to a story he should already be well acquainted with; a story that has been around a very long time; a story that, like an old coat, is well worn and comfortable, lovingly familiar and still entirely useful. In its many pockets we have tried to place little jewels and gifts in order to please and surprise, thereby hoping to encourage the reader to look with fresh eyes and to think again about a subject well worth the time and effort.

Man is a complicated creature, made for the heavens but given charge over the earth. Each man is unique and lives in a unique world within the larger universe that we all share. Our journey through life is really a struggle to understand our world, get to know our selves and so come closer to God. There is a well-known Hadith, "He who knows his self, knows his Lord." God sent us His Books to be our maps and His Prophets and Saints to be our guides. The accounts of the lives of the Prophets are not bedtime stories. They are an important part of the "User's Manual" with which our Most Generous Maker sent us. They have many levels of meaning; told and retold they release new and renewing insights every time they are encountered. They are meant for every age, every time, and every individual.

The story of Moses is a prime example. It is the basis of Judaism, the foundation on which Christianity built, and

Musa peace be upon him.

a cornerstone in the building that Islam perfected. The first five books of the Hebrew Bible, called the Torah in Hebrew and the Tawrah in Arabic, are the Books of Moses. These same five books constitute the beginning of the Old Testament for the Christians. The story of Moses, Musa ﷺ in Arabic, is told throughout The Quran, in over thirty-four chapters. Musa ﷺ himself is mentioned one hundred and fifty-six times, more than any other prophet except the Prophet Muhammad ﷺ to whom the entire Quran is specifically addressed.

The story with which most people are acquainted is usually told from either a Jewish or Christian perspective. However, in this case, the story is told in accordance with Islamic tradition. The first Muslims had no problem learning from the People of the Book who preceded them. Some of the episodes in this story were borrowed early on from Jewish sources and are generally referred to as "Israiliyat" but most of the story stems directly from The Quran and Hadith (sayings of the Prophet ﷺ). The Muslim account of Musa ﷺ differs significantly from the Jewish and Christian accounts in some details and in some interpretations but in its basics it is the same story, told again by a Forgiving Lord to His honored creation. It is believed that The Quran contains the most recent narration of the story of Musa ﷺ and that it is the one meant specifically for this time, for this age and for us.

It would be very superficial to consider the stories of the prophets to be just chronicles or histories that can be proven right or wrong. Whether the Banu Israil crossed the Red Sea or the Reed Sea, whether Pharaoh was Rameses II or Merneptah may be interesting but is beside the point. If the stories are 'unbelievable' or out of sequence or 'illogical' that is because they were meant to be that way. You are meant to understand that they have an existence outside of time. The information they bear is of a different order than you find in history books. This does not mean, however, that they are not real. They are in fact very real on every level. But their physical reality may have been obscured for the purpose of pointing out their higher Reality. Try to understand them, with both your heart and your mind, for what they really are: clues to a higher Truth. They contain the things that God apparently feels His creatures need to know. They will help you to balance your joys and to bear your sufferings.

The Prophet Muhammad ﷺ used the story of Musa ﷺ to encourage his companions to be patient and to persevere. He used it also to lighten his own burdens and to draw inspiration and comfort. There is a Hadith that once after a battle the Prophet ﷺ divided the spoils of war among his companions. One man was heard to mutter against the distribution saying it was inequitable, that one group of people was favored unfairly over another. When he heard about this the Prophet ﷺ became visibly angry, which was a very rare thing for him. Then he said, "May Allah be merciful to Musa. He was injured more than this but he was patient."

In Deuteronomy, the last book of the five considered by the Jews to be handed down to Musa ﷺ on Mount Sinai and written by Musa ﷺ himself, Allah says: "I will raise up for them a Prophet from among their brethren, like unto you (Musa) and will put My Words in his mouth; and he shall speak unto them all that I shall command him." (Deuteronomy 18:18)

This verse without doubt foretells the coming of the Prophet Muhammad ﷺ. His ancestor, Ismail ﷺ, was the brother of Ishaq ﷺ who was the ancestor of Musa ﷺ and the Banu Israil. The Prophets Musa ﷺ and Muhammad ﷺ are the descendents of brothers. There has been no other prophet since the time of Musa ﷺ who resembles him so thoroughly as a lawgiver, statesman, warrior, prophet, and spiritual master.

The Prophet Muhammad ﷺ was given a Divine Book and a new Law, like Musa ؈. He established a new community, like Musa ؈. He suffered the same rejection and opposition from the people to whom he had been sent and, in the end, he had to flee to another country. He spent half his ministry under the oppression of his people, patiently trying to bring them good news. He spent the second half establishing a new nation of believers, governed only by the laws of God. He was destined to show his people the right way in peace and in war. He was a warrior and a judge. There has been no prophet since the time of Musa ؈ who better fulfills this prophecy than Muhammad ﷺ. For this reason, occasionally, the much more detailed and documented story of the Prophet Muhammad ﷺ is used to give insights into the story of his brother prophet, Musa ؈.

At the time the Prophet Muhammad ﷺ first entered Madina he found the Jews who lived in the city to be fasting. He asked the reason for their fast and was told that they fasted in remembrance of the day when God Almighty drowned their enemies in the sea and released them from slavery. Arabian Jews at the time of the Prophet ﷺ remembered their deliverance, by fasting. When the Prophet ﷺ heard this he commanded the Muslims to fast as well, because he said, "We have as much or more right to Musa ؈ as they."

There is another Hadith in which the Prophet ﷺ warned his community, "You shall adopt the practices of the People of the Book (the Jews and Christians) who came before you as closely as the length of a sandal, not missing a step of the way, nor shall their way be any different than yours." Then someone asked, "Will we even worship the golden calf?" "Yes," replied the Prophet Muhammad ﷺ. "There shall dawn upon my community exactly what dawned upon the Banu Israil, as close (in similarity) as the length of a sandal."

The story of Musa ؈ is a teaching story. It contains within its carefully crafted episodes many layers and levels of meaning. It can be read and told to all ages and all cultures and still be understood with ease and enjoyment. If we hope to walk a straight path, if we hope to learn from the past and to be able to catch our missteps before they lead us too far astray, if we hope to find our place in the world, then we must pay attention to the sign posts that our Lord has so generously and so abundantly left for us.

Moses ﷺ in Arabic and Hebrew.

A Prophet Comes To Egypt

Our story begins with the Prophet Yusuf ﷺ. He lived about four thousand years ago in the area generally known as the Holy Land, or Sham, the territory stretching between what is now Syria and Egypt. Technically, Sham is a circle of land with Damascus at its center and a radius the distance a camel can travel in six days. Our story takes place in the southern hemisphere of Sham.

Sayyidina Yusuf ﷺ was born into a long line of prophets: a family of exceptional men who were on intimate terms with their Creator and who navigated the storms of this life with integrity and clarity. Yusuf ﷺ was the son of the Prophet Ya'qub ﷺ, who was the second son of the Prophet Ishaq ﷺ, who was the second son of the Prophet Ibrahim ﷺ. These prophets lived as shepherds, moving their tents as they herded their sheep and camels across the vast pastures of the Holy Land.

The prophet Ya'qub ﷺ had four wives and twelve sons. Two of his wives were sisters, Rahil ؇ and Layka ؇. This was in the time before Allah Almighty forbade a man to have sisters as wives. Ya'qub ﷺ loved and asked for the younger sister, Rahil ؇, but their father Laban tricked him into marrying the older sister first. Because her husband loved her less, Allah gave her more children. Layka ؇ had six sons whose names were Rabil ﷺ, Shakhar ﷺ, Zabalun ﷺ, Shima'un ﷺ, Yahuda ﷺ, and Lavi ﷺ. Rahil ؇ was the younger sister and the beloved of Ya'qub ﷺ. For ten years Allah gave her no children. To compensate for her barrenness she gave her maidservant to her husband to bear them children. Her name was Bilhah ؇ and she had two

Map of Sham.

sons, Dan ﷺ and Naphtali ﷺ. In response to this, Layka ؉ also gave her maidservant, Zilpah ؉, to her husband in marriage. Zilpah ؉ bore him two sons, Gad ﷺ and Asher ﷺ. At last Allah Almighty granted Rahil ؉ and Ya'qub ﷺ children of their own. The firstborn they named Yusuf ﷺ and the second son they named Ibn Yamin ﷺ. Rahil ؉ died shortly after giving birth to Ibn Yamin ﷺ.

These are the twelve sons of the Prophet Ya'qub ﷺ, who was also called Israil. Their descendants constitute the twelve tribes of Israil. All of the sons of Ya'qub ﷺ are said to have been prophets, but in Yusuf ﷺ the light of prophecy shone the most brightly.

Because of the light that radiated from Yusuf ﷺ, the love his father bore him, and the promise of his spiritual ascendancy, his ten half brothers developed strong feelings of jealousy towards him. This made it easy for the devil to whisper in their ears and suggest a plan to get rid of him. His ten half brothers threw him down a deep well and waited to see what would happen. Eventually a caravan came along and, looking for water, they threw their buckets down the well only to draw up a beautiful boy. The head of the caravan decided to keep him to sell as a slave in the slave-markets of Egypt. His ten brothers knew that he was gone by the fact that his light no longer radiated out of the well, lighting up the distant horizon.

In Egypt Yusuf ﷺ was bought by a high-ranking official of the ancient Egyptian court and was raised in his house. After a series of trials and tribulations, he came to be recognized by the King of Egypt, who was later called the Pharaoh, as a most trustworthy and wise counselor. Yusuf ﷺ had an inspiration about what was needed to guard the provision of Egypt and he asked the King to give him the authority to carry it out. But because it is not the way of Allah to give immediately to those who ask, Yusuf ﷺ was made to wait a year before being appointed as Secretary of the Treasury, the guardian of all the wealth and resources of the mighty kingdom of Egypt.

In this high position Yusuf ﷺ discussed all manner of

things with his King and friend. He told him about the religion of Ibrahim ﷺ and Ya'qub ﷺ. He told him that there was only one God Who had created all things, Who was Merciful and Just and Who rewarded His creatures who were also merciful and just. Over time the King came to trust and love Yusuf ﷺ and to believe in what he said. The King of Yusuf ﷺ became a believer in Allah, the one God, and tried slowly to educate his people and to turn them away from the multitude of false gods they were accustomed to worshipping.

After some time there occurred a terrible drought in the land of Sham. From Egypt to Syria little or no rain fell. The pastures dried up. The sheep and goats went hungry. They stopped giving birth and so they stopped having milk. Then they started dying. There was no meat and no milk, the very basis of the shepherd's sustenance. In Egypt also there was drought. The rains did not fall and the river Nile, which supplied most of the water for the agriculture of Ancient Egypt, did not flood and fertilize the fields. But due to the inspired wisdom of the Prophet Yusuf ﷺ the plentiful harvests of the seven previous years had been saved and rationed so that the people of Egypt still had grain in their storehouses. They had enough food for their own people and enough generosity to offer food to their neighbors who were starving.

The sons of Ya'qub ﷺ were among those affected by this terrible drought. They asked permission of their father to travel to Egypt to try to sell what belongings they had and buy food. They were given permission and they traveled together to Egypt. As soon as Yusuf ﷺ saw them he knew who they were, but it took them some time before they recognized him. Yusuf ﷺ treated them with fairness and mercy. They begged him to forgive them and he forgave them. He invited them, with the King's permission, to move their families and to pasture their herds on the rich grasses growing on the eastern lands of the Nile delta.

They returned to their old father, Ya'qub ﷺ with the good news. The family was reunited in Egypt. It is said that they were three hundred and thirteen men in all. They were collectively called by the special name that God had given to Ya'qub ﷺ, Israil, which means 'The One Who Journeys by Night'. The people who moved to Egypt to join Yusuf ﷺ were collectively called the Children of Israil ﷺ, the Banu Israil.

In Egypt they flourished. Their herds grew fat and multiplied. Their women gave birth to many children. The Banu Israil were content and prosperous. They continued to worship God in the way of their fathers and grandfathers.

The King who had befriended Yusuf ﷺ, Rian ibn Waleed, eventually died. In his place there came a new king, Qubus, who was neither a good nor a fair man. He rejected the religion of the one God. He rejected the teachings of Yusuf ﷺ. He returned to the ignorance of his ancestors and ordered his people also to return to the worship of statues and gods with animal faces. He was afraid, because of the love and gratitude that the people felt for Yusuf ﷺ, to turn against the Banu Israil. But he began to hate them because they did not worship him or follow in his footsteps but continued to faithfully walk in the way of their prophets.

Yusuf ﷺ did his best to counsel the new King but to no avail. Eventually he became sickened at the return of the Egyptians to pagan beliefs and he chose to leave this world and return to his Creator rather than be a witness to what they did. Before he died, he called all the believers to gather around him. He blessed them and warned them that difficult times were ahead of them. They must be very strong and patient. They must hold on to the wisdom of their ancestors, to their belief in Allah, their Creator, and to the laws which He had revealed to His prophets.

Yusuf ﷺ warned them that the first sign of the coming difficulties would be that all the white roosters in the land would stop their crowing. They would not crow to signal the dawn or the Morning Prayer. They would not crow to signal the setting of the sun and the Evening Prayer. They would not crow for any prayer or any danger. The white roosters would not crow again until a new prophet was born who would lead them out of their difficult circumstances into a promised land.

3.

The Rooster Of The Throne

The Prophet of the End of Days, Sayyidina Muhammad ﷺ was approached by the Banu Israil of his time and asked forty questions by which they hoped to discover if he was really the prophet they had long been expecting. With the help of the Archangel Jibrail ﷺ, he answered accurately all their very strange and esoteric questions. As a result, all those men of the Banu Israil took his hand and testified to his prophethood. The seventh question that they asked him was to tell them about the "Rooster of the Throne". He related the following:

Above the Throne of God Almighty is a pillar of green emerald supporting a dome of pearl. Standing on the pinnacle of this dome is an angel in the shape of a majestic rooster. This rooster has 500 wings, each of which has one thousand feathers and the color of each and every one of them is pure white. At the five times of prayer this rooster shakes open all of his wings. The branches of the trees of Paradise and all their leaves begin to wave and flutter in the breeze made by his wings. From each feather a drop of mercy falls until it makes a rain of Mercy over the entire world below. The Rooster begins to crow. All the people of the heavens hear this crowing and they ask each other, "What is this good news?" In this way they know that the time for prayer has arrived.

The people of the earth hear nothing but their white roosters cock their heads to one side and listen. Then they begin to flap their wings, and then they start to crow. The other roosters of various colors follow their lead and they also begin to

The Heavenly Rooster.

crow. The people of the world then know that the time for prayer has come. Those who stop what they are doing and get up to pray are bathed in the gentle rain of Mercy falling from the heavens.

The Prophet Muhammad ﷺ said that he likes white roosters, and that his brother, the Archangel Jibrail ﷺ, likes white roosters and that the Lord, Almighty Allah Himself, likes white roosters because they resemble the Rooster of the Throne. A white rooster brings many blessing to the household that owns him both because he is beloved and because he is the first being on earth to hear the call to prayer.

Allah asks the heavenly Rooster why he is crowing. The bird answers that he desires only that his Lord have mercy on the praying people. The Lord tells him that at each time of prayer He looks with the look of Mercy at each of the individuals praying and from that look they become protected from the fires of Hell and are promised the gardens of Paradise. The Rooster of the Throne then at last becomes quiet.

The fact that the white roosters stopped their crowing at the death of Yusuf ﷺ was a sign for the Banu Israil that they were about to be tested and tried. Although they did not know it then, they would be without a prophet for the next three hundred and fifty years. Their prophetic connection with their Lord would be muted. The silence of the white rooster reflected the silence that would arise between them and their Lord. It was now their own responsibility to keep their faith and reliance on God. They would have to turn inward to protect their faith, and be patient. Their resolve and faithfulness were about to be tested.

The cessation of the crowing also signaled that the remembrance of prayer would diminish. The rooster communicated the time for prayer to the world below. Without this reminder the people would find it easier to forget. In consequence the rain of Mercy would no longer fall on the Children of Israil.

Yusuf's ﷺ body was placed in a marble casket according to ancient Egyptian custom, but his people could not decide where to bury him. He was so beloved by everyone that they were afraid fighting would break out over where they laid him. Some say that they diverted water from the Nile, buried his casket in the mud of the original riverbed and then redirected the river to flow back over his resting-place. Some say that they just let the sealed marble casket sink under its own weight into the middle of the Nile. This was done so that no one could disturb his body or move it and his blessing became part of the life-giving river upon which the Egyptian people depended.

משה

3/48

The Fruit Of The Tree

After the death of Yusuf ﷺ the Pharaoh listened to no more advice from the believers of the Banu Israil. He listened only to those closest to him and they were not honorable men. They encouraged his disbelief and his pride. They encouraged him to increase his own power even if that meant being oppressive to his people. They instilled in him a fear of the Banu Israil because they alone of all his people refused to follow him into error.

When King Qubus, who now called himself Pharaoh, died the situation did not get any better, in fact it got much worse. There were two young and clever boys, Walid and Haman, who grew up in Sham, the homeland of Ya'qub ﷺ. They were very ambitious and they decided to move to Egypt in order to seek their fortunes. They began by selling melons outside the gates of the Egyptian capital city. They bought land and opened a cemetery for which they charged exorbitant prices for burial. Together they made so much money that, as is still the way today, they became powerful in the politics of the state as well. Through deceit, dishonesty, and even murder, Walid and Haman took over the highest positions in Egypt. Walid eventually became pharaoh and Haman his closest advisor.

Walid turned out to be even more misguided and tyrannical than his predecessor, Qubus. Maybe in his heart of hearts he knew that his high position was stolen and this gave him a fundamental sense of insecurity. Whatever the truth, he began having dreams that his rule and his kingdom were threatened by the Banu Israil. His closest advisor, Haman, encouraged him

Pharaoh's nightmare.

in this fear. He reminded him that in the traditions of the Banu Israil there was a story about the Prophet Ibrahim ﷺ who had journeyed to Egypt with his wife Sara ﷺ. The Pharaoh of that time had tried to take Sara ﷺ by force to be his queen. God Almighty had prevented this injustice but He had promised the descendants of Ibrahim ﷺ revenge. They were promised that one day they would be placed in a position of authority over the people of Egypt. Haman encouraged Walid in thinking that this would be a political rather than a spiritual victory.

In fact, if properly advised, he should have seen Yusuf ﷺ as the fulfillment of that promise. For Yusuf ﷺ was a great grandson of Ibrahim ﷺ and he had risen to authority over the nation of Pharaoh. Then Walid would have also seen that far from suffering as a consequence the people of Egypt had prospered under his benevolent and wise guidance. Yusuf ﷺ and the rightly guided of the Banu Israil had only offered the best advice and leadership, saving the people from famine and guiding them to the worship of the One and Only God.

One night Walid dreamed that a tree sprouted out of the ground at his feet and grew very quickly to an immense size. From the branches of that tree a great multitude of men were hanging and, like ripe fruit, they began to fall to the ground. These men looked like the men of the Banu Israil. As they landed they started to attack the palace of the Pharaoh. It was as if the prosperity of the Banu Israil was so great it could not be stopped. They were multiplying like fruit, from one tree so many fruit, from one man so many men. Eventually they would take over the country and nothing could stop them. Walid called his trusted advisor Haman to his side and confided in him his fears. Haman suggested that they solve the problem by taking all the wealth and belongings away from the Banu Israil and so chop down the 'tree' he saw in his dream.

In the beginning Walid had only ignored the Children of Israil. Now he began to punish them. He forced them to pay heavy taxes. If they could not pay he forced them into government service. They were required to work many months of the year on building the monuments of the Pharaoh. The Banu Israil were a pastoral people who lived in tents and herded goats and sheep for their livelihood, moving freely as needed from pasture to pasture. The Pharaoh collected them together and forced them to settle in crowded slum-like encampments in order to farm the fields of the king. But still the Children of Ya'qub ﷺ endured and their families grew.

Dreams

The Prophet of the Last Days, Sayyidina Muhammad ﷺ said when he was passing from this world, that he was leaving three things behind him by which his people would continue to be guided. He said these are: The Holy Quran, his own example (his Sunnah), and true dreams. Some believers can occasionally in their life receive inspiration from a dream but a 'true dream' is said to be a fortieth part of prophecy. A 'true dream' is akin to revelation and after the passing of the last prophet, Sayyidina Muhammad ﷺ, it is all that remains of revelation. But, at the time of the early prophets, the time of our story, all people were guided by their dreams and many of these were 'true dreams'. Even the most misguided of them regarded dreams as a true form of inspiration and they paid attention to what they saw. This is why the Pharaoh Walid was so tormented by his terrible dreams and could neither forget them nor ignore them.

One night Walid dreamed that he saw an enormous fire burning in the region of Sham. Terrified, he watched as this fire spread and engulfed all the land that stood before it. Quickly the fire came towards Egypt, until its flames were licking at the golden doors of his very palace. He watched as the fire burned and destroyed all the houses of Egypt, all the inhabitants and their property, leaving only the tents of the Banu Israil. He awoke in a cold sweat. In terror he shouted for his advisors.

Haman suggested to the Pharaoh that he declare himself a god. He had already lived longer than most normal people. He had better health, more wealth, and more power

Pharaoh's second nightmare.

than any other living person. His people already loved him almost as a god. Why not make it official, after all what was one more god? The decree went out to all the people of Egypt: "Your Pharaoh is the god above all the other gods."

Haman suggested that they gather the tribes of Israil to assemble at the palace. The descendants of Ya'qub ﷺ arrived, wondering what was going to happen to them. The Pharaoh sat on his golden throne surrounded by the splendor of his court, in all his worldly magnificence. He demanded that they bow down to him, not only as their king and master, but also as their lord and god.

The men of the Banu Israil were dumbfounded, unable to answer or move. They had changed a lot since their prophet Yusuf ﷺ had died. They had become more and more like their neighbors. They lived in fixed houses, farmed the land, celebrated the festivals of the many gods, drank and partied like all the other Egyptians. But they had not forgotten completely who they were. And there were men among them who kept strictly to the old ways and had forgotten nothing. These men kept the worship of the One God, the Creator of all things. They remembered their prophets and the miracles and favors God had shown to them. These men were unable to bow, unable to serve any God other than Him. Following their lead, not one head, not one knee, not one back among all the people of Israil bent or bowed before the order of Walid the Pharaoh.

In a fit of rage the Pharaoh Walid took away the last rights and property left in the hands of the Banu Israil. They became, literally, his slaves. He divided them into castes. Some were to work without salary in the fields of the king and his nobles. Some were to quarry rocks from the hills. Some were to turn mud and straw into bricks. Some were to dig out the canals and keep the water in them free flowing. Others were to set stone upon stone to construct monuments and public buildings. Slaves of other origins were brought into the houses to do light housework while the Children of Israil did all the hard labor under the blazing sun.

Actually in much of the ancient world slaves were treated relatively humanely and not abused. They were forbidden to move about freely but they were fed and clothed the same as everyone else. The Banu Israil at this time, however, were tormented, over-worked, under-fed, and treated worse than animals. The Pharaoh had over-stepped his limits. He was no longer a righteous king and master who worked for the benefit of his people as a deputy of God. He had become a cruel and tyrannical despot serving no one but himself and his selfish desires. But his most unforgivable crime was to mislead his people into leaving the worship of their Creator and follow him into the error of mistaking the great gifts God had given him - health, wealth, and power - for divinity.

משה

5/48

6.

A Star Is Born

Still the Banu Israil clung to something of their faith and did not mingle completely with the other Egyptians. They continued to be blessed with children who were strong and able to do the work set before them and they continued to multiply and survive. When they entered Egypt with Yusuf ﷺ they numbered three hundred and thirteen. Now they numbered six hundred thousand. "They will one day be mightier and more numerous than we" moaned the Pharaoh. And with these numbers the terror of Walid grew.

He called all the wise men of Egypt to come to his court and study his dreams and advise him on the proper course of action to take. After much deliberation they told him that it was clear that a boy was to be born to the Banu Israil who would grow up to be more powerful than the Pharaoh and more valuable and worthy in the eyes of God than all the people in the kingdom of Egypt put together.

The course of action chosen by the Pharaoh was to prevent the women of Israil from giving birth to any more boy children. He commanded all the midwives of the land to report the birth of any boys among the women of the Banu Israil. If they hid any male births their own lives would be forfeit. According to some accounts the newborn babies were thrown into the river to drown, while their mothers threw themselves upon the banks, their tears intermingling with the already swollen waters. By other accounts the babies were torn limb from limb by the soldiers of the king while their mothers looked on in horror. But by every account, no mercy was shown.

A new star made its shining entry into the night sky.

God says in The Holy Quran that no soul receives any punishment except what it has brought on itself. The Banu Israil had been chosen by God, favored by God with revelation, with books, with understanding.

"And we chose them with knowledge, above all others." (44:32)

Their turning from His way to the ways of ignorance and indulgence did not come without consequences. So although the acts of Pharaoh were without question unjust and tyrannical, the Banu Israil were also not without fault. They had been warned and they, unlike other people, knew and understood. They knew the right way and they chose not to follow it.

What more horrible punishment could be inflicted on the children of Ya'qub ؑ? Did the Pharaoh relent in his genocide? Yes, but not out of remorse, or out of pity, or out of shame. The only reason he relented somewhat was that the people complained that their slave population was diminishing. The old men were dying, the young ones were getting sick and there were no new babies to take their places. Who would hoe the fields? Who would make the bricks? Who would build the walls and dredge the canals? For these reasons, for economic gain only, did the Pharaoh relent in his torment of the Banu Israil. He changed his decree. He condemned the boy babies to be slaughtered in alternate years only. So babies born in one year were fortunate while their brothers, born in the next year, paid with their lives.

Serving in the court of the Pharaoh was one righteous man from among the Banu Israil. His name was Imran ؓ and he was a descendant of Ya'qub's ؑ son Lavi. He remembered the teachings of the prophets, his ancestors, and he clung with fidelity to his belief in God. He had a believing wife named Yuchabad ؓ and two beautiful children, a girl named Mariam ؓ and a boy, Harun ؑ who had been born in a year of good fortune.

Some say that Imran ﷺ, at this point, thought the best course of action would be to divorce his wife, Yuchabad ﷺ, rather than engender any babies for the Pharaoh to kill. His small daughter Mariam ﷺ scolded her father, saying that by this action he would be condemning all the girl babies of the Banu Israil to non-existence just as Pharaoh had condemned the boys. In addition, she reminded him that those souls would not even have a chance to be born, die, be resurrected and go to heaven. At least the baby boys, killed by the Pharaoh, had lived a few breaths. This would enable their pure souls to be received by the Lord in Paradise. Wouldn't it be better, she advised, to trust in God and leave Him to choose death or life for His creation? Imran ﷺ was humbled by her simple wisdom and he kept his wife and resigned himself to accept whatever his Lord decreed.

Now Yuchabad ﷺ became pregnant again and they calculated that the baby would be born in a year in which all boy infants would be put to death. In order to keep her condition a secret, Yuchabad ﷺ stayed in her house and prayed fervently for a girl.

The coming of this child, however, could not be kept a secret from everyone. It is said that when a prophet is conceived in his mother's womb a star, created in his honor, makes its first appearance on the horizon. The wise men, the men of God, know these things and there were those in Egypt who noticed the new star as it made its shining entry into the night sky. Also, those who remembered were elated to hear the white roosters suddenly begin to crow once more. Their joyful sound could be heard throughout the day calling the faithful to prayer. The people of remembrance waited, in fear and in hope, for what was to come.

Nine months later Yuchabad ﷺ felt the first signs of childbirth. She did not call the midwife or anyone to her side. Some say in fact that she was a midwife herself. Her labor was quick and without pain until she saw that the baby she had delivered was a boy. Then her heart burned in her chest and her eyes filled with tears. What was she to do?

"And We revealed to the mother of Musa, saying: Suckle him and, when you fear for him, then cast him into the river and neither fear nor grieve. Lo! We shall bring him back to you and make him one of Our messengers." (28:7)

Yuchabad ؏ was truly a chosen woman of God. For all these many thousands of years she is still remembered and her strength and faith recounted. God mentions her in His Book and says that He 'revealed' to her, a word usually only applied to prophecy. But Yuchabad ؏ was not a prophet. She was a believer and the mother of two prophets. The scholars say that the way in which God gave her revelation was in the same way that He revealed honey to the bee; a natural process resulting in healing and goodness for all humanity. But God alone knows the truth.

Yuchabad ؏ swaddled her newborn and put him to her breast and nursed him until he was satisfied and slept quietly. Then she resolved to keep him hidden as long as she was able, and to obey God. She gave no name to the small baby boy as far as we know but he was a good baby, quiet and still. None of her neighbors guessed that Yuchabad ؏ had had another child. Some say that she nursed him quietly for three months, some say for almost a year, before his cooing and his crying began to attract attention.

Lost

One day Egyptian soldiers came to the house demanding to know if there was a baby inside. Yuchabad ﷺ told Mariam ﷺ to quickly hide him in the oven. The soldiers searched but found no trace of a baby. After they left, Mariam ﷺ ran to the oven expecting the worst but found her baby brother safe and unharmed by the fire. Then Yuchabad ﷺ knew it was time to follow the instructions of her inspiration. For his own safety she must "cast him into the river".

Yuchabad ﷺ was told by God to build for her son a small box out of wood. In the Old Testament, or Tawrah, it is recounted that the baby was placed in a basket made watertight by smearing it with pitch, a tree resin used on boats. But in The Quran, Yuchabad ﷺ was told to have a lidded box made out of wood, just the right dimensions for a baby. In fact it was a little coffin and the Arabic word used for it in The Quran, "tabut," is the same as the word for coffin.

Yuchabad ﷺ went to a carpenter to have the box specially made. The carpenter, however, became suspicious. What was this woman of the Banu Israil wanting with a coffin unless she had a baby to put in it? He knew that he would receive a large reward if he reported her to the king's guards. He went to the palace to try to inform on her but when he got there, his tongue would not form the words. He could only make grunting and slurping noises. The guards threw him into the street thinking he must be either drunk or crazy. Several times he tried to tell someone, but each time, God made his tongue fail him. Finally it dawned on the carpenter that this must be no ordinary request

They rose up alive as the little ark passed over them.

and no ordinary baby.

He returned to Yuchabad 🌿 and asked to know the truth. Fearfully, Yuchabad 🌿 told him the truth and showed him her baby. This baby was unlike other babies. His face shone with the light of Muhammad ﷺ, the light of prophecy, the light of the Promise of Allah. He was perfect in every way, smiling and beautiful. All who saw him felt their hearts open and they could not help but love him. This is the power of attraction, 'jadhba', that Allah gives His chosen ones. Allah says:

"… And I bestowed on you love from Me that you might be brought up under My eye." (20:39)

There is an old story that recounts a conversation between a man of God and Iblis, the devil. The saint asked the devil if he had ever felt love for any son of Adam ﷺ. The devil replied, "I have loved none of them except for Musa ﷺ the son of Imran ﷺ because of the Divine love with which he was endowed."

The carpenter was no exception. His heart opened instantly to the charming infant. He knew of course that this must be the boy about whom the Pharaoh was so worried, and yet he decided to help save him at whatever cost. He constructed the box as Yuchabad 🌿 requested, making it strong and tight and as sea-worthy as a river barge.

By some accounts Yuchabad 🌿 had this casket made soon after the birth of her son. She would nurse him and then lay him to sleep in the coffin instead of in a cradle. She would fasten one end of a long, strong rope to the box and the other end she would tie to a tree on the bank of the river. Then she would let the current take the little craft out onto the wide river far from the dangers of shore.

Every few hours, hiding among the tall reeds on the bank, she would slowly reel in the box. Like most babies in those days he was probably tightly swaddled both to calm him and to prevent active movement. She would nurse her baby until he was full and satisfied. She would gently bathe him in the warm water near the shore before wrapping him up again in his swaddling clothes. Then she would place him back in the 'tabut' and set him in the river to be rocked gently to sleep by its steady current. It might have been possible to continue in this way for even as long as a year. However the time would have eventually come when he was too large and too active to be swaddled and confined to a box. At that time, as much as it must have pained her, Yuchabad ؉ had to complete the orders of Allah.

The time came to do what her mother's heart dreaded most. She must put her beloved son into his coffin and send him off into the dangerous world alone. She might never know if he found the safety of loving arms to cradle him or if he drowned and was eaten by crocodiles, or was lost forever among the tangled stems of the lilies of the Nile. Even though Allah's promise was clear, that He would bring the baby back to her, the actual act of putting him into the river took all of her courage and tested her heart to the utmost. Even this strong believer, chosen among women to give birth to two prophets and to be inspired with God's comforting words, wavered in her obedience.

Yuchabad ؉ padded the inside of the 'tabut' with the best bits of soft fabric she could find, hoping to make it look like the cradle of a noble baby rather than that of a slave. Then quickly, before she could change her mind, she laid her precious child inside and fastened the lid. She untied the rope and pushed the little craft into the big river. She watched as the current carried him swiftly out of sight. She called her daughter, Mariam ؉, and told her to run along the bank and to not lose sight of the box, until she saw its final resting place.

Every mother can sympathize with Yuchabad ؉ as she let her child go upon the river. Every mother must at some point let go of her child, to stand on the sidelines and watch as he follows his own destiny, hoping that one day God will bring him back. But Yuchabad ؉ had to give up her baby, not her grown child, to the vagrant currents of the world. With her own hands she had to put him alive in his coffin, trusting that God, his Creator, would care for him and bring him back safely. We can take strength from her enormous strength and inspiration from her divine inspiration.

The little ark sailed along the river, literally and symbolically, over the bones and rotting corpses of the thousands of baby boys who had been sacrificed because of him. It is written that his father, Imran ☘, had had a dream in which he saw all the dead children, lying at the bottom of the river, rise up alive as the little coffin passed over them and they sang joyfully the praises of their Lord. For in all truth this coffin held, hidden inside of it, real life, the possibility of eternal life, for all the believers of the world. Some say that the strength of all those pure little boys entered into the chosen baby as he passed over them, making him stronger and more pure than any single mortal. Their sacrifice had not been for nothing. All of their pain and missed opportunity was in fact to be redeemed and fulfilled in this one baby boy.

$$\frac{7}{48}$$

8.

Found

The little ark had not traveled far before it was swept into a quiet canal that channeled water from the mighty river to irrigate the gardens of the king. The Pharaoh Walid had built a beautiful palace and surrounding garden for his favorite wife whose name was Asiya ☙ or Bithiah in Hebrew. Some say that Asiya ☙ was of the Banu Israil. Some say she was a princess descended from the legitimate Pharaohs who had ruled before Walid and Haman. She was lovely and, most importantly, she was a believer. She was certainly one of those called "hanif", those noble men and women who without following any particular religion have a rightly guided sense of Truth and are led by Allah directly to His Way.

The Pharaoh also had a daughter from another wife, whom he loved very much, who had been afflicted since childhood with a very serious disease. All her body was covered with sores and open wounds. The doctors of ancient Egypt were very knowledgeable even by today's standards. They were able to perform all kinds of delicate surgeries, skilled in the arts of herbs and healing energies. But not one of these doctors was able to do anything to relieve her suffering. At some point in desperation the Pharaoh had consulted a soothsayer, a wise person who sometimes could predict the future. This soothsayer had told them that a creature in human form would emerge out of the river Nile from between two pieces of wood. No one had any idea what this might mean but because they had no other hope, the queen, the princess, and their serving girls used to walk the banks of the beautiful river every day hoping to chance

The little ark was carried to Pharaoh's palace.

upon this creature.

This particular day the Queen Asiya 🌿, her husband, Pharaoh Walid, and his daughter were walking together, enjoying the garden and the fresh breezes coming off the river, when they spotted something bobbing about in the canal. Asiya 🌿 commanded her serving girls to dive into the river and bring it to them. After a short swim the girls could be seen pushing in front of them a little wooden coffin with the lid tightly shut. The girls were afraid to open the box so they just pushed it before them in the water.

When they reached the shore it took several of them to carry it and set it before the Queen. Asiya 🌿 pried open the top and found inside, to her great surprise, the most lovely, healthy, smiling baby boy. Now Asiya 🌿 was a very young and beautiful woman but her husband, although strong and healthy, was not a young man. He was as hard and cruel as she was sweet and loving. He was as deceitful and calculating as she was honest and innocent. It had not been a happy marriage for her but she knew it was her destiny and she could perhaps control the Pharaoh enough to prevent him from doing more injustice to the people. No matter what potions they drank or practices they endured they had not been able to conceive a child. This was a source of much heartache for the Queen. The Pharaoh had had many children by many other wives but he truly loved his young queen and wanted a child, if only for her sake.

He was greatly surprised to see her smiling and clapping her hands in joy at what she saw in the box. He was expecting it to be some dirty thing or decaying corpse. Both the Pharaoh and his daughter came rushing to Asiya's 🌿 side to see what was in the coffin. They also were surprised and delighted to see a lovely baby boy peering up at them. The Princess bent over to pick up the child. In doing so she knocked out of his mouth the fingers on which he had been happily sucking. The saliva on his baby fingers smeared over her arm. Immediately the sores covering that arm were gone, healed and vanished. The Princess cried out and began rubbing the saliva of the child over every inch of her body.

While she was doing this, Asiya ﷺ held the baby in her lap, feeling his warmth, breathing in his sweet smell, and slowly falling in love with this radiant child. The Pharaoh also seemed to be enchanted with the boy and of course marveled at the instant cure of his daughter and the unusual happiness of his Queen. This ended abruptly when Haman appeared. He sourly ignored the happiness in the scene before him and reminded Pharaoh of what should have been already obvious – the baby must be the cast-off child of some criminal woman of the Banu Israil. The baby must be killed, immediately.

Asiya ﷺ and the princess held on to the baby, begging for his life. Asiya ﷺ kept her considerable wits about her. She had experience dealing with her husband and his advisors. She did not argue about the origins of the child, his true origin was obvious. Instead she said: This is not the child of the Banu Israil who was predicted to threaten the Pharaoh. This child is the one in the prophecy having to do with the healing of the Princess: two completely separate prophecies, two completely different babies.

"And the wife of Pharaoh said: Maybe [he will be] a consolation for me and for you. Do not kill him for he may be of use to us, or we may choose him for a son." (28:9)

The Pharaoh looked at his Queen holding the baby as if it were her own, tears running down her beautiful cheeks and although probably in his heart he knew the truth, he consented to her keeping the child and raising him as her own. But he was not happy and no longer looked with affection on the tiny boy. It is said that if Pharaoh had submitted then to the truth he knew in his heart, that beautiful baby would have truly been a consolation for him as well as for his Queen. But turning away from the truth, turning away from the light, Pharaoh sealed his own fate. Allah says in The Quran:

"And the family of Pharaoh took him up, that he might become for them an enemy and a source of grief. Lo, Pharaoh and Haman and their hosts were ever sinning." (28:8)

Pharaoh was being clearly shown that not only was he not a god and had no power to prevent the Will of his Lord, but that Allah Almighty could produce the foretold boy and arrange to have Pharaoh, knowingly, accept him and raise him in his very own household. Even a warning and advance notice could not prevent the fulfillment of Allah's decree.

$$\frac{8}{48}$$

Returned

Now Asiya ﷺ had permission to keep the lovely baby boy but she needed to make preparations for caring for him. He was hungry and his tears tore at her heart. She called all of the women working at the palace who were nursing children. She offered a large salary for any one of them willing to take on this baby and nurse him along with her own child. Most of the ladies of the court wanted to be chosen as wet nurse to the child who could possibly be the future king.

The relationship between a wet nurse and her foster baby constituted a lifelong bond. The child continued to call the woman, mother, and the woman called the child her son. It was a common practice at the time for women other than the birth mother to nurse an infant in return for money. This practice was still in place at the time of the birth of the Prophet Muhammad ﷺ some twenty-five hundred years later. This practice probably began for the health of the child. It is a known fact that some women make better milk than others, richer, higher in nutrients, and sweeter. The Prophet Muhammad ﷺ had a nursing mother, Halima as-Sa'diyya ﷺ to whom he showed respect and love all of his life. He called her, mother, and her children his brothers and sisters. In Islam it is even forbidden for children nursed by the same woman to marry just as if they were true brothers and sisters. The bond of milk is similar to the bond of blood.

Not one of the women at the court was able to nurse this baby however hard they tried. He would not suck at the breast of any one of them and his crying became intense. Asiya

Mariam had been hiding in the reeds by the edge of the river.

🐝 grew frantic. But this was Allah's plan.

"And We had previously withheld from him all wet nurses." (28:12)

Allah did not allow this baby to drink from any of the Egyptian women of the court of the Pharaoh. The baby Musa 🕊 could not take nourishment from any but a woman of belief. It was not possible for him to take sustenance from unbelief.

Asiya 🐝 was desperate. She had tried all options. She did not know where to turn. At this moment Mariam 🐝 managed to arouse enough courage to reveal herself and speak. She had been hiding in the reeds by the edge of the river all this time, marveling over the events unfolding before her eyes. In an instant her baby brother had gone from foundling, cast on the river in his coffin, to prince and inheritor of a great kingdom. Fearfully, but guided and determined, she stepped out of the bushes and made her presence known.

She was a young girl and she spoke innocently and sweetly, her voice full of genuine concern. She knew of a woman, she said, living nearby who had just lost a child and who was known for her good milk and her caring ways. She would probably be happy to take the Queen's 🐝 child and show him all the affection and care the Queen 🐝 could desire.

"Shall I direct you to a household that will feed him for you, while they are sincere to him?" (28:11-12)

The King and Queen 🐝 were surprised by the offer of this unfamiliar child and questioned her extensively. Finally satisfied that she was telling the truth and only trying to help, they told her to bring the woman quickly to the garden where they sat.

Mariam 🐝 ran as fast as she could back to her house to call her mother to the Queen 🐝. Yuchabad's 🐝 heart raced. Allah's promise was true. Yuchabad 🐝 grabbed her shawl and hurried to the palace with her daughter. There in the Queen's 🌿 arms lay her beautiful baby, safe and dry, hungry but otherwise as perfect as she last saw him. Allah says in The Quran:

> "And the mother of Musa's (Ummi Musa) heart became empty of everything. She would have disclosed [the truth] about him if We had not strengthened her heart, that she might be among the believers."(28:10)

Her heart became empty of everything but her child and her love. She forgot Allah's promise and might have betrayed the trust He had put in her, so great was her longing to grab her son in her arms and declare that he was hers. But her heart was strengthened and she kept her head. She took the baby on her lap and began to nurse him. He hungrily drank and drank until he was completely satisfied and went peacefully to sleep.

The Queen 🌿 and her ladies were surprised and began to wonder if maybe this woman was in fact the natural mother. But Yuchabad 🌿 kept her head and explained to them that she was known for her good milk. All her children had been healthy and plump and all babies were happy to drink from her milk. The Queen 🌿 wanted to believe her and they began to negotiate the terms of their contract to feed the newfound prince.

The Queen 🌿 wanted Yuchabad 🌿 to move into the palace. She offered to give her an apartment on the palace grounds, and many other wonderful luxuries. But Yuchabad 🌿 felt strong now in her knowledge of God's support and she negotiated cleverly. This served to convince the royal couple finally that this woman of the Banu Israil was not the mother but simply an unrelated woman interested in making the best deal and getting rewarded for service to the king.

Ummi Musa 🌿, now secure in her position of strength and divine support, refused all efforts on the part of the Queen 🌿 to convince her to move to the palace. She had other children to care for. She insisted to remain in her own house and take the prince with her. Once a week she agreed to bring him to his adopted mother, the Queen Asiya 🌿. This was a great triumph because it meant not only would she have the freedom to educate her son in the ways of her people, the Banu Israil, but he would also grow up familiar with his brother and sister.

The Prophet Muhammad ﷺ treated his nurse, Halima as-Sa'diyya 🌿, as his mother to the end of his life and honored all her children and even her whole tribe, for her sake. So the child Musa ﷺ would probably have had legal and emotional ties to Yuchabad 🌿 that were recognized by all. In this instance it meant that the family, and also the neighborhood, of Yuchabad 🌿 were spared much of the harsh treatment dealt out to the other members of the Banu Israil. The labor required of them was lighter and more humane. In this way he immediately became a blessing to the larger community.

משה

$$\frac{9}{48}$$

10.

Names

The son of Yuchabad and Imran now became officially the son of Pharaoh Walid and his Queen, Asiya. They needed to choose a name for him. The name by which he is known to this day is Moses in English, Moshe in Hebrew, and Musa in Arabic. Some say that this name comes from a Hebrew word meaning to draw out, moshe. The Queen drew him out of the water. But she would have been unlikely to give him a Hebrew name and even if Ancient Egyptian and Hebrew are related languages the baby was the one taken out of the river not the one doing the taking out as implied by the form of the word.

Arabic scholars say that the name Musa is of Ancient Egyptian derivation. 'Mu' means water and 'sa' means wood. He came out of the river in a wooden box. According to the prophecy he was the human creature pulled out of the water between two pieces of wood. This makes sense and is accurate. But there is another understanding as well. In Ancient Egyptian, 'moses' means, 'son of'. It was used in Egyptian names in much the same way that Ibn is used today in Arabic or Ben in Hebrew. Muhammad Ibn Abdullah means Muhammad son of Abdullah. Soloman Ben David means Soloman son of David. So the name Tutmoses means the son of the god Tut. Ramses is really Ramoses or son of the sun god Ra. Musa was named by his Egyptian parents an Egyptian name indicating that he was their son, or the son of one of their gods if part of the name is missing.

The name Musa is his real name. It is the name by

The Arabic names of Musa, Harun, Asiya, Walid, and Pharaoh.

which Allah Almighty addresses him at their first meeting at the site of the burning bush and then subsequently at other times.

"And when he reached it, he was called by name: O Musa! Lo I, even I, am your Lord." (20:11-12)

Pharaoh, on the other hand, is the title given to every king of Egypt since the New Kingdom, about 1400 BCE. Pharaoh means "Great House". It is a title of respect given to the king indicating that he is the house, the safety, the shelter, for his nation. He was considered the father of his people, their creator and god. In The Quran Pharaoh is referred to twice as "The Possessor of the Many Tent Poles" (38:12) (89:10). The more tent poles there are, the larger and more magnificent the tent. Therefore, even in The Quran Pharaoh is addressed as Possessor of the Great House. The ruler of Egypt at the time of Yusuf ﷺ is not called by the name pharaoh in The Quran. He is simply called malik (king), which indicates that the story of Yusuf ﷺ took place before the fifteenth century BCE when the rulers of Egypt were still kings and not gods.

The personal name of Pharaoh is not used in The Quran or in the Tawrah; Allah always refers to him only as Pharaoh. He was the ruler of Egypt and the representative of God to his people, "the shadow of God on earth." This is why he was expected to be just and generous to those he ruled. We are told that for the most part Pharaoh was just and generous to his own people and that may be why Allah continues to give him respect with this title of honor even though he was not a believer. The other tyrants mentioned in The Quran, such as Nimrod, are called by name not by their titles of honor.

In the old chronicles the personal name of the Pharaoh at the time of Musa ﷺ was said to be Walid. In Arabic the root of this word means 'born' or 'son'. It is interesting to note that both Musa ﷺ and Pharaoh have essentially the same name. They are simply known as mortals, the sons of man.

The name and identity of Haman has aroused a lot of

controversy since the Middle Ages. He does not exist in the Bible or Torah. It is now thought that "haman", like "pharaoh" was not a personal name but a title. HMN (the vowel sounds are not known) in Ancient Egyptian represented the word for slave or servant. The High Priest, the chief advisor to the Pharaoh, was called "the Servant of God" (HMN-NTR). It is probable that Haman was the man who occupied this most influential postion at the time of Musa ﷺ.

The name of Harun ﷺ, in Hebrew Aharon, means "bringer of light" or "lofty mountain". True to his name he assisted his brother in bringing the light down from the mountain of Sinai, the Tawrah down from the highest heaven. It must have been inspiration for his parents to give their firstborn son such a name. The light on the mountain is a perfect symbol of the prophethood of both Musa ﷺ and Harun ﷺ.

The Quran does not name the mother of Musa ﷺ. It only refers to her as Ummi Musa ﷺ, Mother of Musa, which is the name of honor that Allah bestowed on her. The name Yuchabad is mentioned only in the Tawrah. In Hebrew they say it means " Yahweh honored her". "Yu" represents Yahweh, and "kabit" means honored. However, God was not called Yahweh by the Banu Israil at this time. God tells Musa ﷺ His sacred Name for the first time later in the story. Perhaps it is the name given to her later in order to honor her high station. But another reading of her name is "Yu-khividh" which means 'strong'. Then her name means "God gave her strength". In The Quran, God says,

"if We had not strengthened her heart, that she might be among the believers." (28:10)

Allah strengthened her heart, steeled her heart, so that she would have the courage to throw her baby in the river and then still have the control not to betray her overwhelming love for him when he was returned to her.

The name of Asiya ﷺ, the wife of Pharaoh, means

caregiver. She was someone who took gentle care of the weak and helpless. She fostered the small abandoned baby and loved him as her own. In the stories of the Banu Israil they name her Bithiah, which means daughter of God in Hebrew and say she was the daughter of Pharaoh rather than his wife. It is thought, that some pharaohs did actually marry their own daughters but many wives were called daughters simply in order to increase their rank. The fact that she is called daughter of God could be a testament more to the strength and sincerity of her faith, rather than to her ancestry.

11.

Pharaoh's Beard

Little Musa ﷺ was raised in the house of his mother Yuchabad ؋, his father Imran ؋, his older sister Mariam ؋ and his older brother Harun ﷺ. No one knows for sure the period of his nursing but it was probably at least two or three years. Some chroniclers say that he might have lived as long as ten or fifteen years with his family of birth. However long, the day finally came when Asiya ؋, the Queen, asked for her son to come live with her permanently in the palace. Ummi Musa ؋ prepared the boy. She washed and oiled him. She dressed him in the cloth of gold Asiya ؋ had given her. As she did this she might have softly recited the Hebrew prayers that she had sung to him every day of his life and hoped in her heart that he would remember who he was. She kissed him and gave him up for the second time in his short life.

They received the young Musa ﷺ with great ceremony at the palace. The palace guards, dressed in golden cloth, decorated with plumes and tassels, were lined up to salute him. The servants of the palace formed another line and they bowed and knelt before him. His many relations stood to greet him holding expensive gifts and burning incense. He was the little prince, the son of the god Pharaoh.

His adoptive mother, Asiya ؋, took him by the hand and led him to her husband, Pharaoh Walid. The Pharaoh took him in his arms and raised him high so all those assembled could see him. He was about to present this child to the court as his heir when Musa ﷺ stretched out his small arms and took two handfuls of Pharaoh's beard and pulled with all his might. For

Two platters were brought, one of rubies, one of glowing coals.

such a small boy he was quite strong. Delighted and laughing, he lifted up his pudgy fingers, which were now entwined with many long hairs from the beard of his father, the god Pharaoh.

Pharaoh's face showed his anger and he handed the boy quickly back to his mother and cursed him. Haman, as always ready by his side to give bad counsel, swore that the boy must be the one of Pharaoh's dream, the one come to destroy him. Quickly Asiya 🍃 protected her child. She told the king that no small child has enough understanding to form a strong intention. The boy was just playing; he intended no harm. This story points to the probability that Musa 🕌 was somewhere between five and seven years old, when conceivably a question might remain as to whether he was still innocent of calculated action.

To see who had the right interpretation, Haman or Asiya 🍃, a test was devised. Two platters were to be brought, one containing bright shining rubies from the treasury of the King. The second held glowing coals from the palace ovens. They were both to be shown to the child. If Musa 🕌 chose the rubies he would show that he had sense and could be considered accountable for his actions. If he reached for the coals this would demonstrate that he was still an innocent and could not be held responsible for what he did.

The platters were brought, each one glowing red and sparkling with light. Musa ﷺ began to reach for the jewels, but the angel Jibrail ﷺ was dispatched by Allah to intervene. He forced Musa's ﷺ little hand to reach for the burning coals. Musa ﷺ picked up a live coal in his hand and put it to his mouth. Asiya ؇ screamed and knocked it out of his hand but it had already done its damage. The hand and tongue of the child were severely burned.

This story would explain why the Prophet Musa ﷺ had difficulty speaking and being understood. Later in life Musa ﷺ complained to the Lord that his speech was unclear and he needed his brother's help to communicate the Divine message clearly. And Pharaoh, when Musa ﷺ had come to declare his prophethood, mocked his inability to speak clearly. The story would also explain why the fact that his hand became white without defect would later be a great miracle or sign. Pharaoh would recognize that all the scars of this childhood incident had been wiped away.

But there is another version of this story. When Musa ﷺ reached out his hand to touch the rubies, the Archangel Jibrail ﷺ forced his hand to go instead to the coals. Pharoah, seeing the boy's tiny hand approaching the glowing coals, snatched away the bowl and prevented any injury to the child. Asiya ؇ then understood that Pharoah's enmity towards the child did not arise from ignorance. He knew the child, he knew his destiny, and most importantly, he knew the One who had created both. And it is of this crime, denial of the Truth, that Pharaoh was guilty.

Allah used the life of the Prophet Musa ﷺ as an example for the Prophet Muhammad ﷺ and his companions. The story is told and retold in The Quran many times. There were also times when the companions sat together and discussed the stories in the company of the Prophet ﷺ. After his death, they continued to recount the stories among themselves with the explanations and interpretations they had heard. The recounting of these conversations, as they were remembered, is collected in the

Hadith. A cousin and companion of the Prophet ﷺ, Ibn Abbas ؓ, related one of the most important series of Hadith on this subject. He was approached many years after the death of the Prophet ﷺ and asked to recount the story of Musa ؑ as he had heard it told at the time. He told the story of the life of Musa ؑ as a series of tests or trials. This set of Hadith is collectively referred to as 'al Futun' – the Trials.

The first trial was that he was conceived and born in a year in which the Pharaoh had condemned all the male children of the Banu Israil to death. The second trial was being almost killed when he was discovered by Pharoah and Haman. The third trial was waiting for his mother to be chosen as his wet nurse. The incident of choosing between jewels and coals was the fourth trial of his childhood.

11/48

12.

Growing Up In Two Worlds

We know little to nothing about the life of the Prophet Musa ﷺ from the time he was a toddler until he was forty years old. There is one verse in the Holy Quran that addresses the result of his adolescence and early manhood. In the New Testament there is also one sentence: "And Moses was educated in all the wisdom of the Egyptians and he was mighty in words and deeds." (Acts, 7:22). This period of his life is not mentioned in the written Tawrah. Although there are a few stories in the Talmud and Midrash, none of them were taken up by the Muslim scholars. Most of what follows is based on supposition; the bare outlines of the most probable circumstances of the youth of this most remarkable man.

Musa ﷺ was raised as a son of the king of the richest, most powerful nation of the time. Egypt was the agricultural capitol of the ancient world and this allowed for the development of cities and large urban areas. It had had a stable government for centuries. All of this meant that there could be people who did not have to grow or raise their own food. Religious men, scholars and scientists, doctors and artists could be supported by the larger society. It was a stable and peaceful society where people from all over the world could gather and contribute. Learning and art flourished. There were even two universities in Egypt at the time, one in Heliopolis, and one in Memphis where it is believed that Musa ﷺ was raised.

At the supposed time of Musa's ﷺ birth, the kingdom of Egypt had been in existence for over two thousand years.

As he went between the two worlds the Truth must have been clear.

The pyramids were already one thousand years old. The great cities and temples of Aswan and Memphis were thronging with people. Most of the greatest of the pharaohs had already reigned. Egypt had colonized much of the Middle East and Africa. It had a large army and powerful ambitions. Its capital, Memphis at the time Musa ﷺ probably lived, was the center of wealth and learning for most of the world.

But perhaps the most astonishing aspect of Egyptian life was its emphasis on the after-life. All the art, architecture, learning, and wealth were focused on preparing the living for what awaited them after death. On the east bank of the Nile the people built their simple houses of mud brick and farmed their fields, even as they do today. Of this little trace remains. But on the west bank, the bank of the setting sun, they built their temples and religious institutions, buried their dead and immortalized their kings. Here they built with carved and quarried stone. Here they built monuments meant to last an eternity.

In general the Egyptian kingdom was benign and believing. It was orderly and law abiding, wealthy and generous. It worshipped a variety of gods but recognized the existence of One God, the Creator of everything. The other gods could be understood to be the representations of the many attributes of the one God. For such a wealthy and powerful society, its emphasis on eternal life, rather than on the ephemeral pleasures of the life of this world, was unique in world history.

One can only assume that Musa ﷺ was a handsome and intelligent boy and that his adoptive mother provided him with the best of everything Egypt had to offer. Some believe that he was trained as a high priest and became adept in the mysteries of the ancient religion. Some believe that he was trained as a warrior and led an army to the conquest of the city of Meroe in Ethiopia.

It is said that he married an Egyptian woman and had two sons. It is also said that he married the Ethiopian queen and brought her to Egypt. He accompanied his father, the Pharaoh, wherever he went, whether sailing on the Nile or sitting in judgment in the public council. He was an accepted member of the royal court. Wherever he went he was treated as an heir to the kingdom, a prince of Egypt.

He had been educated by the best minds of his adopted nation. He knew the secrets of astronomy and astrology. He knew mathematics and music, geometry and architecture. He knew the history of the kings of Upper and Lower Egypt, the course of their battles and the extent of their victories. He knew the gods of Egypt: Horus, the god of the sky with the head of a hawk; Thoth, the god of knowledge with the head of an ibis; Anubis the god of the dead with the head of a jackal. He knew their names, their stories and their supposed powers.

He had called on these many gods in their sacred temples and he had been unanswered and unmoved. He had watched the priests lay sacrifices on their many altars and he had seen nothing and heard nothing. But even in that place, there must have been true believers among the priests and devotees of the many gods. Every religion is founded on a true revelation. Beneath the panoply of animal headed gods rested a deeper, truer, primordial knowledge. All men must remember when they existed in the world of souls and they stood before their Lord and Creator and He asked them, "Am I not your Lord?" All of the souls of every human who ever lived or who will ever live answered "Bala, yes indeed." (7:172) There must have been those who remembered and worshipped the one God, beside Whom there is no other.

In the house of Imran ؎ and Yuchabad ؎ he saw them pray to this God without statues of gold and silver, without costly temples constructed by slave labor, without a privileged class of priests and their politics. He listened to their prayers in a language foreign and beautiful and he understood and he learned, and his heart opened. As he went back and forth between the two worlds the comparisons must have been obvious and the truth clear. How could he consider Pharaoh, his foster father, a god and worship him? He could see with his own eyes that he was cruel

and unjust. He was petty and petulant, insincere and selfish. He ate and drank and used the toilet. He was undistinguished by any godly trait other than worldly power.
Allah says in His Quran,

"And when he (Musa) reached his full strength and was ripe, We gave him wisdom and knowledge. Thus do We reward the good." (28:14)

This verse follows the story of Musa's ﷺ nursing and is the only verse that addresses his growing to manhood. It tells us three things. First, Musa ﷺ was given 'hukm', which is wisdom in the sense that he was able to judge right from wrong. Second, Musa ﷺ was given knowledge, 'ilm', which implies that he did not just have knowledge but he had a correct understanding. And third, that he was good: he was moral and ethical, kind and compassionate, all the characteristics we associate with goodness.

He had never been touched by unbelief. Even in his nursing as a baby he refused to drink the milk of the unbelievers. We can assume that just as Allah had protected him from being nourished by unbelief as a baby, He protected him from being sustained by unbelief as a young man. His adoptive mother, Asiya ؔ, is mentioned in The Quran as one of the two most saintly women ever created. She was his shelter and his companion as he grew up in the palace. There were other believers among the people of Pharaoh and they must have been of much comfort and companionship to each other.

And as he matured his certainty also matured inside of him. Whether as the Jewish accounts tell, he joined his brother Harun ﷺ in traveling and teaching in the encampments and villages of the Banu Israil, or he helped as he could the Hebrew people who were within his neighborhood by keeping the authorities from abusing and mistreating them. To whatever extent, their torment must have been lightened by Musa's ﷺ presence among them. He was too kind and wise to tolerate injustice. He was too strong and brave not to be obeyed. He was the son of the king but his heart lay with the slaves.

All the prophets found a ready reception among the poor and disenfranchised of their nations. The wealthy, established in power, either thought they already knew everything or were afraid of change. This made most of them deaf to truth. The poor were broken already with nothing to protect or to lose. They heard the call of Allah's messengers and responded wholeheartedly. The majority of the first followers of the Prophet Muhammad ﷺ were from among the very poor, the young, the women, or the slaves. This was the reason his family criticized and ridiculed him. They called him a prophet of the weak and worthless. The Prophet Salih ﷺ was the crown prince among his people but he chose to uphold justice and to work and live among the poor. The same is true for the Prophet Isa ﷺ.

We do not know at what point Musa ﷺ was made aware of his true origins and birth. But he knew Imran ﷺ and his family and was comfortable in their home. He knew his brother Harun ﷺ well enough to know his talents, abilities, and his trustworthiness. Later he would ask Allah to appoint Harun ﷺ as his helper, in particular because he knew him to be an eloquent speaker. Little by little the differences between the sincerity and humbleness of Imran ﷺ and the arrogance and ignorance of Pharaoh must have become all too apparent. The differences between the social, political and economic conditions of his two families must also have weighed heavily on him. For almost forty years Musa ﷺ lived like this, a prince and a slave, with a foot in both worlds.

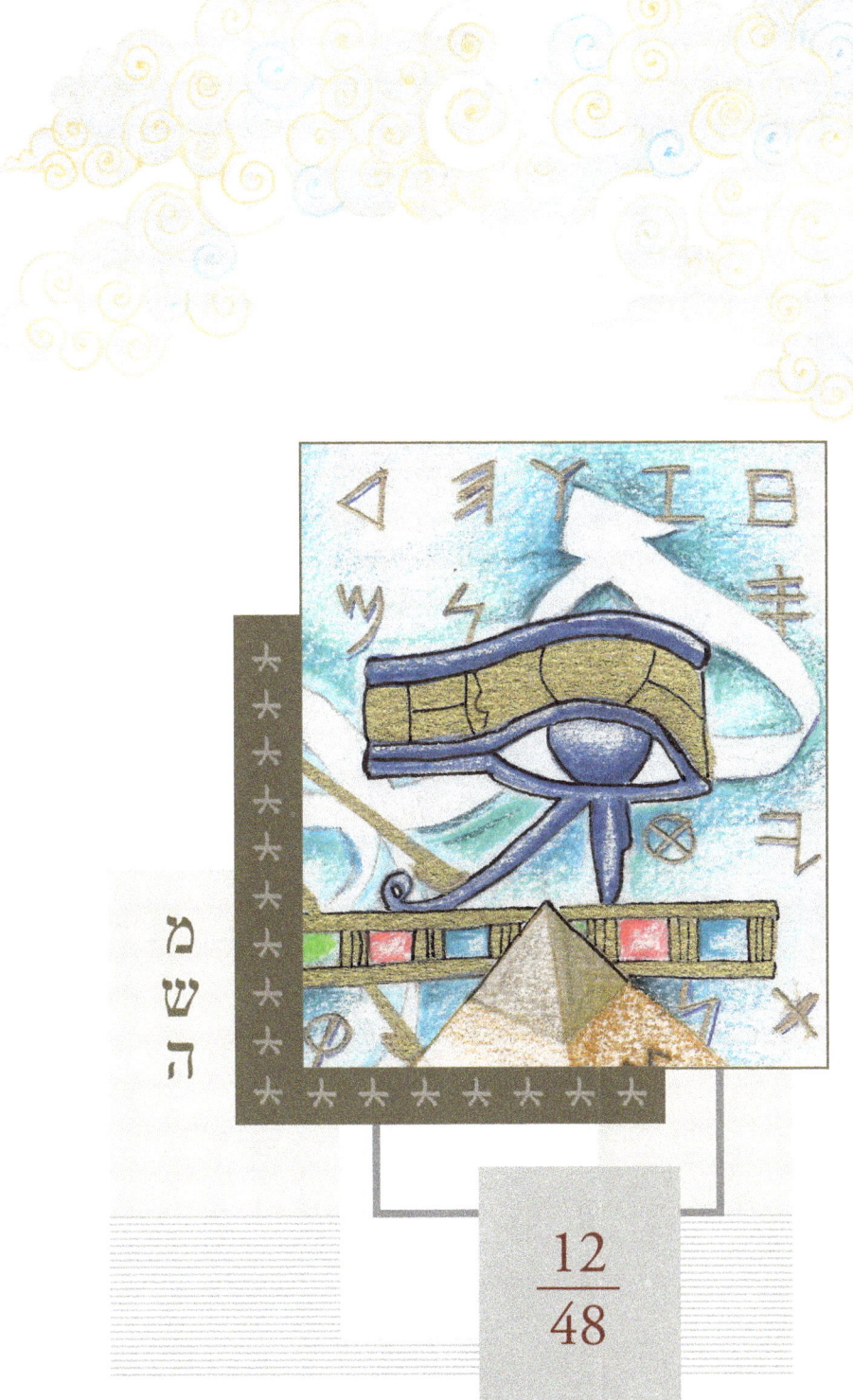

$$\frac{12}{48}$$

13.

A Life For A Life

One day, in his thirtieth year, Musa ﷺ was forced to make the choice between his two worlds. It was the time of day when the people of the city lay down their tools and retreated into the shade of their houses and gardens to rest and nap. It was at a time when the streets were empty and no one was around. Musa ﷺ was walking alone on the street when he saw two men fighting. By their dress he knew them to be an Egyptian overseer and a man of the Banu Israil.

The Egyptian was severely beating the slave and Musa ﷺ reacted quickly to the injustice apparent in the situation. He either stepped between the two men in order to stop the fight or he took the side of the slave who he thought was being abused. In doing so Musa ﷺ pushed the Egyptian hard on the chest. Some say that the strength of the Prophet ﷺ was so great because of all the souls of the infant Banu Israil that were gathered together in him. Some say that he was trained as a military man and made perfect in strength by God. But certainly a man acting with the authority of God and motivated only for the service of God is given Divine strength. God supports his action with His Strength. God knows best. But the push that was only intended to separate the two combatants ended up killing the Egyptian. It is said that the hand of Musa ﷺ actually passed through the chest of the angry overseer and killed him instantly.

Musa ﷺ was horrified. The man of the Banu Israil was terrified. They both ran from the scene in different directions. Since there was no one else about in the streets there were no other witnesses to the accident. Musa ﷺ went to his home. He

Forgive us Allah Almighty.

may have acted with the power given him by Allah, but he had taken a life and in that he recognized the hand of the devil.

"This is of satan's doing. Indeed he is a clear, misleading enemy. He [Musa] said: My Lord! Indeed, I have wronged my self, so forgive me." (28:15-16)

He begged his Lord to forgive this dreadful deed. It had not been his intention to kill the Egyptian, only to stop the fight. He had no motive other than compassion and the desire for justice. But a life had been taken in the heat of the moment. Allah says,

"We decreed for the children of Israil that whoever kills a human being for other than manslaughter or corruption in the earth, it shall be as if he had killed all mankind, and whoever saves the life of one, it shall be as if he had saved the life of all mankind." (5:32)

The action was an accident and it had been motivated by the desire to prevent harm rather than to cause harm. It certainly was intended to stop corruption and injustice. Allah forgave him right away. But Musa ﷺ did not absolve himself. He vowed that never again would he be an associate or supporter of the guilty.

When the authorities discovered the body of the dead

Egyptian they found no indication of who committed the murder and no witness. It would have remained that way except that when Musa ﷺ was out walking the following day he saw the same man of the Banu Israil fighting with another Egyptian. Musa ﷺ stepped up to him, horrified that he had committed such a grievous sin to protect a man who was simply a hothead and a troublemaker. The man recognized Musa ﷺ, saw the anger on his face, and was afraid that Musa ﷺ was going to kill him this time. Without thinking he said, "Do you intend to kill me just as you killed the Egyptian yesterday?" This time the streets were crowded and all the people heard the man identify Musa ﷺ as the murderer of the Egyptian guard.

Musa ﷺ was not sure what to do. He set out to return to his home, to wait there for whatever would happen. But The Quran says that a man came running from the other side of the city warning him that the officials had been apprised of his guilt and that he had lost royal support. He would be hunted down like an ordinary criminal for a crime against the state. He advised Musa ﷺ to flee the country for his life. This man is not identified in The Quran. Some say it was the carpenter who had built the box for Ummi Musa ؑ so long ago. Some say it was a believer who, like the Queen Asiya ؑ, was a member of Pharaoh's family.

The day before, by defending the slave against the slave driver, the oppressed against his oppressor, he had killed a man. Today he was made to realize that the oppressed was also guilty. In this case justice was illusory. In this fight there was no justice; he was both the oppressed and the oppressor. He had made a solemn vow never again to support the guilty. He was now without recourse. He had nowhere to turn. Everything partaking of this world was guilty. He put away all worldly things and turned his face completely towards his Lord, the only place in which justice actually exists.

"And when he turned his face toward Madyan, he said: Maybe my Lord will guide me to the right road." (28:22)

Musa ﷺ fled from the city into the desert. He left his family, his children, his home, everything he had ever known or loved. He left his identity, and the promise of his future. He left behind the world, as he knew it, and his self, as he knew it. He oriented his heart towards God and became a stranger and a wanderer on the face of the earth. This was the fifth trial of Musa's ﷺ youth.

$$\frac{13}{48}$$

14.

A Stranger

When Musa ﷺ left his home that morning he had no idea that he would never return. He had only gone out for a walk. He was wearing the Egyptian waistcloth and some soft sandals on his feet. Now he had no idea where to turn, nor in what direction safety lay. The believer who had come running to warn him advised him now to leave the main roads and the expected destinations and to set out into the desolate uninhabited wastelands. Musa ﷺ raised his hands and he prayed to his Lord, saying,

"Perhaps my Lord may guide me to the sound way." (28:22).

It is said that Allah sent two Archangels to guide him, Jibrail ﷺ and Mikail ﷺ, who appeared to him as men. Jibrail ﷺ led the way so that Musa ﷺ would go in the direction his Lord willed, and Mikail ﷺ rolled up the road behind them so that no one would discover a trace of their passage.

Some say that the journey of a month was shortened in this fashion to a couple of days. Others say it took eight days and eight nights. Some Jewish sources claim that the journey was a trial and a training that could have lasted even as long as 40 years. Muslim scholars posit that this journey was the first khalwat, or spiritual seclusion, of the Prophet Musa ﷺ. For at least forty days he journeyed without material provision and without any intention other than total reliance on his Creator. The Prophet Muhammad ﷺ said, "He who devotes himself

Jibrail ﷺ led the way and Mikail ﷺ rolled up the road behind them.

exclusively to God for a period of forty mornings, the fountains of wisdom will spring forth from his heart and upon his tongue."

Musa ﷺ traveled east, past the Red Sea to the Sinai and then to the southern end of the peninsula. He avoided villages and stayed off the well-traveled trails. He ate what wild plants he could find and the leaves of trees. He drank from the occasional rocky pool. All the time he beseeched his Lord for guidance.

According to Islamic Shariah, the sentence for one who kills another man by mistake is to pay recompense to the family of the dead. But if the killer is unable to pay then he must fast for two months. The prophets hold tightly and strictly to the law of God. It is probable that Musa ﷺ fasted at least this amount of time on his grueling journey to Madyan.

He crossed the Gulf of Aqaba and entered the Land of Madyan. Musa ﷺ arrived, worn out, barefoot, and hungry. He had had no cooked food since leaving Egypt. His sandals had long ago broken and been discarded. They say that he walked until he had even worn through the soles of his feet. At Madyan he found a well and drank his fill and then lay in the shade of one of the neighboring trees to rest, thin and exhausted. Ibn Abbas ؓ said that because he had been subsisting solely on leaves and plants, the green color of his intestines was visible through the thinness of his skin.

He slept a little and when he awoke he found a crowd of men encircling the wells in the process of watering their animals. The men were noisy and rough as they shouted at each other and at their animals. The thirsty goats and sheep were bleating and baaing as they pushed to get to the water first. The whole scene was one of turbulence and chaos. Musa ﷺ noticed two young girls standing with a small flock to one side of the general commotion. The shepherds began to taunt and tease them until it appeared that the girls might be in physical danger. Musa ﷺ stepped in to force the shepherds to stand back.

Although he was tired and weak he asked the girls politely the reason they were not watering their animals. Of course he realized that they were shy and modest and so unable to enter the rough crowd of men but he thought they must have a brother or father somewhere with them. They answered him quietly that they were alone; their father was too old to accompany them to the well. Usually they watered late in the day after the men had left but today they had come too early. Because the men sealed the wells with huge boulders after they were done, usually the girls had no recourse but to water their flock on the muddy dregs the shepherds left in the troughs.

It was then that Musa ﷺ noticed a second well nearby with a big boulder placed over the top to ensure that no poor traveler could help himself to water. He lifted the boulder easily despite his weakened condition. It is said that it usually took several men to lift the boulder that covered the well but Musa ﷺ lifted it without difficulty. He then set about hauling water with their leather bucket and dumping it into the trough for the goats to drink.

The animals drank their fill, and the girls filled their water skins. Then they gathered the flock together and left for the tent of their father some distance away. Musa ﷺ lay back down in the shade of the acacia tree and said,

"My Lord indeed I am in need of any good You might send me." (20:24)

Musa ﷺ did not ask the girls for payment or charity. He helped them only to please his Lord and now he asked only his Lord for help in his desperate situation, whatever help He chose to send.

After some time Musa ﷺ saw one of the girls returning to the well. She spoke to him shyly at some distance, saying that her father had asked her to return to invite the stranger who had watered their flock and protected them to come for dinner. Musa ﷺ was greatly relieved by this most kind invitation. He rose to follow her. As they walked, a strong wind came up across the desert in the late afternoon and it blew at the girl's skirts as she walked ahead. Musa ﷺ turned his eyes away but he noticed her embarrassment and discomfort. He asked the girl to walk behind him; she could point out the path by throwing a stone in the right direction whenever there was a choice. By doing this, her modesty was protected from even his unintentional glance. In this fashion Musa ﷺ and the girl arrived at the tent of her father some distance away.

14/48

15.

Shuayb ﷺ

The shepherd girl was named Saffura ﷺ, or Zipporah in Hebrew, which means little bird. She was the oldest daughter of the Prophet Shuayb ﷺ and a descendant of the Prophet Ibrahim ﷺ. Allah Almighty had sent Shuayb ﷺ as a prophet to the people of Madyan and Aykah. He was called Shuayb, because it means, one whose heart is on fire with the love of God.

For many years Shuayb ﷺ had advised the people of Madyan to correct their ways. Just as they blocked their wells from being used freely by the passing stranger so they were greedy and dishonest in all their dealings. They lived alongside a mountain pass and they had turned this into their livelihood. They unfairly charged travelers a tax for just passing through their land. Often they demanded that the travelers sell to them at reduced prices. In their market places it was common to find the scales falsely balanced so that an unfair advantage went to the merchants of Madyan.

Everyone knew they were liars and thieves, but they had no defense against them. There was no other way to travel through the mountains and their market places were well frequented and large. Shuayb ﷺ was a big man with a large voice. He was given the gift of eloquence and his preaching was magnetic and convincing. After some time the authorities of Madyan arranged to have him evicted from their city because his arguments were too persuasive. Many of the poor and victimized were taking courage from his sermons and demanding their rights.

Shuayb ﷺ abandoned Madyan but his Lord did not

All the unbelievers were reduced to ashes.

give him permission to abandon his mission. He was ordered to continue preaching to both cities of Madyan and Aykah. He settled in a place near the main road that led from one city to the other. Every day he stood on a boulder beside the road and beseeched the travelers to listen to the word of Allah, to listen to His guidance to the path of righteous living and good sense. He was an imposing figure, as he stood high on the rock, his long beard and turban blowing about wildly in the turbulent air rising from the valley below, his large, deep voice carrying firmly over the sound of the wind, his lids tightly shut over his half blind eyes. Many travelers stopped to listen and some understood and accepted. They brought his teachings back to their own countries. But the people of Madyan accepted nothing and continued to ridicule him and ignore his warnings.

After many years, the people of Aykah also rejected him and united with Madyan to expel Shuayb ﷺ from their territory altogether. Only then did Allah inform His Prophet that the time for divine punishment had arrived. The sun drew near until it filled the sky and scorched the earth with its heat. The people could find no shelter. Even a large dark cloud, that gave the appearance of providing shade, only increased the heat. The people of Aykah were roasted alive in their homes, as in an oven. All the unbelievers of the city died and were reduced to ashes that were blown about by the wind and mixed with the dust, until nothing remained of their existence.

The people of Madyan were hit with an earthquake that took them by surprise in the night. It shook their houses until the walls shattered and the roofs fell down. For their pride they were buried under the rubble of their extravagant buildings and then the earth opened up and swallowed all trace of them.

Many of the honest poor did follow the prophet Shuayb ﷺ, however. They joined him finally and moved to a new land near what is now Mecca and there they lived out their lives and were buried.

At the time of our story, however, Shuayb ﷺ was still living in the vicinity of Madyan and trying with all his power, to inform them about the one God. He was old and he was tired and partially blind. He had no sons, and no companions had moved with him at this point to his exile outside the city. His two daughters were his only help and all he had.

Each day these young girls took their small flock of sheep and goats out to pasture and every three days they brought them to the wells of Madyan to give them water. But the evil inhabitants of Madyan had placed large boulders over the mouths of the wells, which took four of their men to move. The girls were unable to uncover them on their own. So they waited until after the shepherds of Madyan had watered their numerous animals and then they shyly crept up to water their small flock on the dregs of water left in the troughs. The male shepherds would give them a hard time, tease them and be rude to them.

On the day that Musa ﷺ arrived, tired and hungry, the shepherds had been particularly rough and rude. Only the presence of a stranger, Musa ﷺ, had protected the girls from their advances. After watering their herds the shepherds had made sure to dump all the water out of the troughs and to roll the boulder back in its place. The girls would have had no water that day and no chance to draw any of their own.

So Musa's ﷺ kindness and superior strength had been much needed and was very much appreciated. He rolled back the boulder by himself, without help. He drew buckets of water from the well and quenched the thirst of the animals. The girls had rushed home, earlier than usual and full of complementary descriptions of the emaciated stranger who had come to their aid and had asked for no favors in return.

Shuayb ﷺ was heartened to hear their tale. It had been a long time since anyone in that country had shown any act of generosity or unsolicited kindness. He invited the stranger to join them for a simple meal, hoping to find a friend and companion with whom to share the wisdom of God

Shuayb ﷺ sat the stranger down and offered him food and drink. He thanked him for the help he had given his daughters. Only then did Shuayb ﷺ ask Musa ﷺ what chain of events had brought him to Madyan, a stranger, barefoot and hungry. Musa ﷺ kept no secrets but told the venerable old man his whole story. After hearing the tale, Shuayb ﷺ told him that he had no need to fear for his life any longer. Madyan was out of the range of the Pharaoh and his men. Musa ﷺ had prayed, on the day he turned his back on Egypt,

"My Lord save me from the wrong-doing people!" (28:21)

Now Shuayb ﷺ answered him,

"Do not fear. You have escaped from the wrong-doing people." (28:25)

Shuayb ﷺ explained that he was a descendant of the prophet Ibrahim ﷺ and a believer in the one God, a follower of the prophets. He was not Banu Israil because he was not a descendant of Ya'qub ﷺ, who was also called Israil. He was, however, a descendant of the Prophet Ibrahim ﷺ and a prophet himself in his own right. Like his ancestor Ibrahim ﷺ, it was the custom of Shuayb ﷺ not to sit down to a meal unless he had a guest to share it with him. He welcomed Musa ﷺ, as a distant cousin, to stay with them as long as he wished.

Saffura ﷺ had been the one who had told her father of the generosity of the stranger at the well and who had been sent back to invite him to come for dinner. Now she was inspired to say to her father,

"O my father, hire him. Surely the best one you can hire is the strong and the trustworthy." (28:26)

Shuayb ﷺ liked what he saw in his guest, his humble manner and truthful speech. He recognized a believer in Musa ﷺ and was prompted by God to make him a generous offer.

Shuayb ﷺ offered him one of his beautiful daughters as a bride. If Musa ﷺ accepted, Shuayb ﷺ would wave the customary bride price and Musa ﷺ could serve him as a shepherd for eight years, or maybe ten.

"Indeed, I desire that one of these, my two daughters, marry you on the condition that you hire yourself to me for eight years. If then you complete ten, that will be from your side, but I do not want to put you into difficulty. You will find me, God willing, among the righteous." (28:27)

Musa ﷺ had found a new home. Divinely directed, he had made his way through the wilderness to the hearth of another man of God, to be trained further and protected until his own mission would be delivered to him. He had put himself in the hands of his Creator just as when his mother had put him into the river. And Allah had brought him out in safety. He consented to the proposal. He chose Saffura ﷺ, whose kindness and modesty he had already noticed and admired. She was the one who had spoken well of him to her father and had been inspired to suggest that they hire him. To speak well of someone is a form of charity. To her great joy Musa ﷺ asked her to be his partner in marriage.

משה

15/48

16.

A Shepherd's Staff

So the agreement was made with Allah as witness. Musa ﷺ would take Saffura ؑ to be his wife and would work for eight years shepherding the sheep and goats of his father-in-law Shuayb ﷺ. At the end of that time, if possible, he would continue herding for Shuayb ﷺ for another two years. Then he would be free to take his wife and move somewhere else to make a life of his own.

Before Shuayb ﷺ could send Musa ﷺ out with the flock he needed to provide him with the one tool that a shepherd requires, a shepherd's staff. Shuayb ﷺ had a few of them in his tent. He asked his second daughter to fetch one for Musa ﷺ. Saffura's ؑ sister went into the tent and brought back a wooden staff. Shuayb ﷺ took it and felt it with his hands because his eyes no longer saw well enough to identify it. He said no, it was not the right one and to bring him another. According to some traditions she brought out each staff one by one, but her father became confused. He could no longer tell the difference between them and so, not being sure, he rejected all of them. Frustrated, in the end, he gave Musa ﷺ the first staff his daughter had handed him.

According to other accounts he sent Musa ﷺ in to choose a staff for himself. Musa ﷺ chose the first one that came readily to his hand, but Shuayb ﷺ refused to give it to him. Each time Musa ﷺ went in to take another, only the same staff made its way into his hand. Shuayb ﷺ kept refusing to give the one he brought until both men were aggravated and upset. Finally he relented and let Musa ﷺ take it.

It was the staff that Adam ﷺ had brought from Paradise.

Musa ﷺ set off with the animals but he had gone only a short distance when he heard his father-in-law calling and saw him blindly stumbling down the path after him. Shuayb ﷺ could not find it in his heart to part with that particular staff. He explained that the staff Musa ﷺ had chosen was no ordinary one, it had been given to him in trust by an angel of God. It was the original staff that our ancestor, the Prophet Adam ﷺ, had cut from a myrtle tree that grew in the garden of Paradise.

According to other accounts the first tree to be planted on earth came from a seed that Adam ﷺ had carried down from Paradise. The tree was what we call a boxthorn and from it Sayyidina Adam ﷺ had cut a staff - this very staff. The staff was as tall as a man and forked at the top. At the bottom end it had a hook. It had been given to Shuayb ﷺ to keep until the next prophet, to whom it was destined to belong, would come to claim it. He was told that this prophet would be one of the greatest prophets who would ever live and he would be known as 'the speaker with God - Kalimullah'. At this time there was no indication that Musa ﷺ was that chosen man and so Shuayb ﷺ felt morally impelled to withdraw his gift.

Musa ﷺ was fed up with all the indecision about the staff and anxious to get started on his day's work. This time he refused to give the staff back to his father-in-law. They actually started to fight over the staff when a stranger happened to pass by. The stranger advised them to throw the stick on the ground and whoever could pick it up and raise it the highest would show himself to be the true owner. Neither Musa ﷺ nor Shuayb ﷺ thought this a very clever idea since the stick was not heavy or hard to lift, but they agreed to the stranger's idea because they were desperate to avoid further argument.

When Shuayb ﷺ tried to lift the staff he found it exceedingly heavy. He was only able to raise it a few inches off the ground. Musa ﷺ, however, lifted it easily over his head. It became quite apparent to them both that the stranger was not an ordinary man, just as the stick was not an ordinary stick. Shuayb ﷺ let Musa ﷺ take it and the man, who was actually an angel, informed him later in secret that he had, in fact, fulfilled his trust and delivered the staff to its rightful owner.

It was the custom of the men of the past to give names to the weapons and tools that served them well. The Prophet ﷺ had a sword named al Adb, and another named al Ma'thur. He had another sword named al Battar, which is in the Topkapi and is said to be the one Sayyidina Isa ﷺ will use when he returns for the last battle at the end of time. Sayyidina Ali ؈ had a famous double bladed sword whose name was Dhul Fiqar. It is related that the staff of Musa ﷺ also had a name. One companion related that its name was Masa. Another said that he had heard that it was named Naf'ah, meaning 'useful'. Another companion said that he had heard its name was Ghiyath meaning 'help'. And a forth said its name was 'Ulayq, which means 'twining shrub'.

It has been written that this staff had many special powers. If Musa ﷺ hung his bags from its hook the staff proceeded to travel behind him like a pack animal. At night it glowed like a torch and lit the way through the darkness. It had a voice and kept him company in the wilderness. If it was stuck into the ground it sprouted roots and branches and bore delicious fruit. If an enemy appeared the staff defended its owner and Musa ﷺ had no need to lift a hand. But only Allah knows the truth and it seems that, at least at this point, Musa ﷺ had no idea just what kind of powers this simple stick might have.

Musa ﷺ took his flock out into the countryside to look for pasture. In this way he was to spend the following ten years. Alone in the wilderness with the stars for company, he contemplated the majesty and grandeur of his Lord, by watching and learning from the signs of His creation. He was literally immersed in the pages of the Book of Creation. And so in this way he became absorbed also in the author of that book – Allah Almighty.

A good shepherd needs many skills, of most of which city people are both ignorant and oblivious. He needs to know the topography of the land and the kinds of herbage it provides. He needs to be able to read the signs of the coming weather. He needs to be able to find his way by means of the stars. All of these skills, and many others, must have been quite new to a man raised to be a prince of Egypt. Musa ﷺ had much to learn before Allah Almighty could entrust him with the care of His people, to be their shepherd and guide.

Musa ﷺ learned to pasture the flocks of the Prophet Shuayb ﷺ faithfully and with care. He kept them safe from wolves and lions. He guided them across rocky wastes and through mountain passes into the greenest valleys. He watched the sky and learned to recognize the signs of rain in order to lead them to faraway mountain pastures. He read the seasons and he knew the fields so that he could guide his flock to the best grass at the right time. He ran up the steep sides of ravines to coax them down and headed them off before the sudden precipice. He woke with them in the morning and went to sleep with them at night. He ate the berries and the grains produced by the same plants the animals ate. He led them to water in hidden pools and drew water for them from the deepest wells. He, in turn, drank their warm, foamy milk.

He learned to know his animals by face and by personality, as do all good shepherds. The young ones he led to the new grass, lush and green, easy for them to eat. The older ones he led to the taller grasses they preferred. The strongest ones he let forage on the trees and brush, pulling down branches with his staff for them to gnaw on. He knew which animals were rebellious and needed a firm hand, which animals were gentle and easily scared. He knew which animals were leaders and which ones needed prodding. He knew which ones were sure to always head for trouble and which only wanted to return home. His Lord watched him and saw that he gave to each animal its rights and to each its needs.

When he saw a young one struggling to keep up, his heart softened and he raised it to his shoulders to ease its journey. He delayed the whole flock to wait for the older, slower ones. His Lord saw all this and was pleased. If Musa ﷺ had such compassion for a small animal he would surely be gentle with the people placed under his care.

The Prophet Muhammad ﷺ said that all of the prophets spent a period of their lives serving as shepherds. It is an appropriate occupation for a man who will one day be the shepherd of men.

משה

16/48

17.

The Fire That Did Not Burn

Musa ﷺ finished his eight years of service to Shuayb ﷺ. He agreed to complete the longer term of ten years because a prophet always keeps his word to the fullest extent and does the best and the most of what he is able. In appreciation for his service and as a charity for the small family, Shuayb ﷺ told Musa ﷺ that any lambs born neither white nor black but of mixed color in that tenth year would belong to him and Saffura ﷺ. With Allah's blessing all the lambs born that year were twins of mixed color.

Saffura ﷺ had given birth to one son, Gershon, and was pregnant for a second time when the ten years were finished. A great longing arose in the heart of Musa ﷺ to retrace his steps across the barren wastes and hidden valleys of the Sinai through which he had fled so long ago. He asked permission of Shuayb ﷺ to take his wife and children, the animals that he had acquired and the shepherds who had attached themselves to him. He set out to fulfill his destiny. It is said that his intention was only to visit Egypt in secret, to sneak into the city of his birth and see Asiya ﷺ and his parents, his wife and children, and then leave again immediately.

He took with him tents for shelter, some food and water. He took his fire drill, which was the way they made fire before there were matches. And, of course, he took his trustworthy staff. They traveled by day, and at night made camp. Musa ﷺ would set up the tents and light a fire with his fire drill. Then they would cook a meal of milk and wild grains. They slept by the fire both for protection and warmth because the desert in

He saw a tree that appeared as if on fire.

winter can be very cold. At some point a storm blew in. There was dust and wind and rain. It grew cold and dark. They kept traveling but because of the darkness and wind they lost their way. They had to make camp and wait for a clear night sky to reveal the stars that would guide them back to the right way.

Try as he might in the fierce wind, Musa ﷺ could not get the tents to stay erect nor could he get a spark from the fire drill to light. His wife began to feel the pangs of labor with their second child. The little family huddled in the wilderness, in the cold and dark, unable to prepare food or find adequate shelter from the elements. Musa ﷺ prayed fervently to the Lord for aid and for guidance.

Then all of a sudden Musa ﷺ saw in the far distance a flame shoot up, cutting through the darkness. His heart leapt. Where there was fire there should be people. They might be able to help him with directions, or at least give him a burning brand to carry back to his family to start a fire. So he took leave of his wife and headed out into the darkness to find the light.

As he got closer he noticed something unusual about the flame. It did not flicker or waver; it neither died down nor did it spread. After walking some more, he arrived at the base of a mountain. There he saw quite clearly a bramble bush or stunted acacia tree glowing with a bright light that made it appear as if it were on fire. But clearly the branches were green and not burning. The light radiated out and its rays rose high up into the heavens. Musa ﷺ approached cautiously. There were no people around. It was unlike anything he had ever seen before.

Every time he got close, the flame drew back, away from him. Every time he drew back, the flame shot forward as if to grab him. This happened several times until he was gripped with intense fear. But his immediate purpose was not to benefit himself; it was to take care of his family and those who depended on him. They needed the fire. He could not give up or run away. He steeled himself. He picked a handful of green leaves and approached the light. He thought if he could only collect a burning coal he could carry that back to his encampment. At the very least they would be warm and could make something to eat.

This time, as he approached, he heard a voice, and it was calling him by name. The voice said,

"O Musa, indeed I am Allah, Lord of the worlds." (28:30)

He was so astonished that his legs buckled under him and he fell to his knees. The voice was soft and reassuring and called him to approach closer. His heart beating wildly, he pulled himself slowly to his feet, using his staff as a brace. Allah sent two invisible angels to support him on either side and, thus aided, he took several steps closer to the burning bush.

The voice was like nothing he had ever heard before, but somehow familiar. Still Musa ﷺ trembled with fear. The majesty of the sound, the radiance of the light, the awesomeness of the scene, brought the mighty shepherd to his knees. Who was this? What was happening to him? Was it God he was hearing or was it satan? Even the Prophet Muhammad ﷺ after seeing Jibrail ﷺ for the first time, went back to his wife, Khadija ﷺ, afraid that maybe he was delusional or going mad.

It is reported that someone once asked Musa ﷺ how he knew that the voice belonged to his Lord. He answered that the voice of a person is heard only by the ears and comes from a single direction. He heard this voice with every inch of his body and as if it were coming from all directions at once, both inside and outside. The voice assured Musa ﷺ,

"Blessed are those who are in the fire and whoever is around it. And glory to Allah, Lord of the worlds. O Musa, indeed it is I – Allah, the Mighty, the Wise."(27:8-9)

He was reassured that this was a blessed meeting and all connected with it were good and holy. In the Tawrah Allah identifies Himself at this point in Hebrew as YHWH, four consonants that have been translated as: "I am the One Who is". The consonants without vowels make the Divine Name unpronounceable, consequently keeping it both sacred and untouchable. Vowels were added later to make the name Yahweh, which is sometimes rendered as Jehovah. Muslims interpret this name as "YaHu" in Arabic, which translates similarly as "He Who is". In The Quran, however, the Divine Voice identifies His sacred name as Allah.

"O Moses, indeed I am your Lord, so take off your sandals. Indeed you are in the sacred valley of Tuwa. And I have chosen you, so listen to what is revealed. Indeed I am Allah. There is no god except Me, so serve Me and establish prayer for My remembrance." (20:11-14)

The Prophet Muhammad ﷺ called Musa ﷺ "Najiullah" – the confidant of Allah. The Almighty, beyond description, beyond understanding, beyond every beautiful, marvelous, glorious comparison, the one God, was talking in a familiar way to His humble servant, the shepherd of Madyan, Musa ﷺ son of Imran, Musa ﷺ son of Pharaoh. He had chosen him from among all the souls and all the creatures He had made.

Just as the Muslims of today take off their shoes when entering the mosque or any holy place, Musa ﷺ was asked to do the same for this most holy valley in the desert of Sinai, the place where he met with his Lord. But we also take off our shoes when we enter our houses. Taking off the shoes symbolizes getting comfortable, taking our ease, coming home. Just as Musa ﷺ lost his Egyptian sandals when he fled from Pharaoh and went barefoot into the wilderness, taking off shoes symbolizes a change from one state to another. His sandals now represented his spiritual state as a wanderer, a stranger, a seeker of God. Taking them off represented the fact that this phase of his life had ended; he had arrived at his destination. What he had been seeking had found him. He was no longer a stranger and a traveler. He took off the last, dirty traces of his ego and became a perfected soul.

The education and training of the Prophet Musa ﷺ took place in four stages. His intellect and reasoning were sharpened in the centers of Egypt. He grew into a learned and cultivated man. He was forced to abandon all that and be purified in the desert of loss and despair. From being a prince he became a servant, a servant to a servant of God. Finally he became a servant to one of the lowliest creatures of God, a herder of sheep. Gradually he had learned both the inner and the outer forms of God's religion. Allah had directed his education in every detail up until this point when He informed him,

"You came to this place as I decreed, O Musa, and I have chosen you for Myself." (20:40-41)

God had chosen Musa ﷺ to be His Prophet and His Messenger.

$$\frac{17}{48}$$

18.

The Hand And The Staff

Musa ﷺ stood his ground in his bare feet and faced the voice of his Lord coming from the firelight surrounding the green tree on the right side of the mountain in the sacred valley of Tuwa. No one can know the terrible majesty and wonder of this meeting. Only one prepared, as Musa ﷺ had been prepared, could hold his ground and remain lucid and sensible within the immensity of this manifestation. Then the Most Merciful Lord asked him a very mundane and surprising question,

"And what is that in your right hand, O Musa? It is my staff" Musa ﷺ replied. "I lean on it and with it I bring down leaves for my sheep, and I have other uses for it." (20:17-18)

The Lord of the Universe asked a simple question and Musa ﷺ replied in a simple manner. He used this staff every day in his shepherding duties; to herd the sheep, to pull down the branches of trees for them to eat from the leaves, to beat the tall grasses and bushes, and to rest against during his many hours of standing and walking. These were mundane tasks that the Lord of all the Worlds would certainly already know. But this staff was to play a very important role in the story that was to follow. And this was something about which Musa ﷺ did not know but was about to learn. Musa ﷺ did not know the other uses for this miraculous staff that he had inherited from Adam ﷺ, that had been protected by angels and given to him by the Divine Will from the hand of another prophet.

He threw the staff and it became a serpent moving swiftly. (20:20)

Allah ordered Musa ﷺ to throw the staff on the ground. When he did this it transformed unmistakably into a serpent, hissing and spitting and whipping itself around in the sand, moving very swiftly. The forked top of the staff had become the vicious open jaws of the serpent. The hook on the end had become a fin on its spine, waving menacingly back and forth. Some say it became an enormous python that proceeded to swallow whole, a nearby tree. Some say it was a dragon of fearful proportions. The prongs became jaws with twelve fangs and a molar tooth that screeched as flames shot out of it. Its eyes flashed like lightning strikes. Whatever it touched it torched. It would swallow boulders as big as camels and the broken pieces could be heard rattling inside its belly while it smacked its lips, hungry for more.

Musa ﷺ was completely taken aback and turned to run. In fact he did run and would not have turned or even looked back if he had not heard the voice addressing him again. Allah ordered him to return and not to fear. The voice commanded him to grasp the serpent by its jaw and promised that it would transform back again into its original shape.

But Musa ﷺ was hesitant to grasp this terrifying creature with his bare hand. First he wrapped the end of his woolen cloak around his hand thinking to protect it. But again he was commanded not to fear. He was clearly ordered to put his bare hand into the mouth of the serpent, into the mouth of fear itself. He overcame his horror and reached out and grabbed the serpent by its open jaw. In his hand he found his familiar staff. It had transformed back into his most useful and necessary tool. This staff was to be a sign and so was the hand that held it.

The Prophet of the Last Times, Sayyidina Muhammad ﷺ, said that when he was a small boy pasturing his flocks in the hills and valleys of Arabia an angel came to him, laid him on his back and cut open his chest. The angel took his heart out of his body and washed it in a basin of clear water from the pools of paradise. The Prophet ﷺ said that a small black spot washed off his heart. This spot was fear. Fear is the weakest point of the human heart. The devil uses this fear to catch and manipulate humanity. Fear of death drove our ancestors Adam and Hawa ﷺ to follow shaytan, to eat from the forbidden tree and be expelled from Paradise. Fear of failure, fear of shame, fear of loss, fear of change, fear of the unknown, all our fears drive us to seek reliance on other than God. Without fear the Prophet ﷺ was safe. Shaytan did not have a means to reach him.

Musa ﷺ now accomplished this same feat. By facing his fear, by standing up to it, it became a tool in his hand and he was safe from the temptations of the devil. The staff became a symbol of the Truth against which nothing false can stand.

"O Musa, approach and do not fear. Surely you are of those who are secure. Put your hand over your heart and then bring it out white and shining. And guard your heart from fear. These are two proofs to Pharaoh and his men. For surely they are an evil doing people." (28:31-32)

Now Allah asked Musa ﷺ to put his hand into his shirt and bring it out white and without defect, shining like the moon. Some say that the prophet had leprosy and he put his hand to his heart and brought it out healed. Some say that he was a brown skinned man and that the skin of his hand turned white as if he had leprosy. Some think that this was the hand that struck down the Egyptian and it was forgiven and made white as a sign of its innocence.

Some say that choosing the glowing coal as a toddler in order to deflect the anger of Pharaoh had scarred his hand. Its whiteness indicated that the skin of his hand had been restored and the scars eradicated. This would definitely have been a sign that Pharaoh would have recognized. Musa ﷺ was a man, chosen, purified, and perfected by God Almighty. He did not have leprosy or any disease and it is unlikely that he had any serious handicap. He was perfect in mind and in body.

There is a story that took place later in his life that supports this second opinion. The Prophet Musa ﷺ, like all of his fellow prophets, was very modest and proper. When the other men gathered to bathe together in the river, Musa ﷺ would not join them. Instead he would find a private place and bathe alone by himself. The men of the Banu Israil began to wonder at this unusual modesty. Some among them began to suggest that their prophet was maimed or disfigured in some way and had something to hide.

One day when Musa ﷺ had retired modestly to a secluded place to bathe, he piled his clothes on a dry rock by the edge of the water. Allah caused the rock to awaken and move away from its place, taking with it the clothes of the Prophet ﷺ. Musa ﷺ finished his bath and reached out to the rock to retrieve his clothing. Only then did he notice that the rock had grown feet and was running away. Without thinking Musa ﷺ sprang out of the water and ran after the lively rock in full view of his people. In this way the Almighty put the suspicions of the Banu Israil to rest and showed them that their Prophet ﷺ was indeed whole and perfect in every way.

As for the murder of the Egyptian, it was an unintentional act caused by Musa's ﷺ unparalleled physical and moral strength. It was the effect of the righteous anger aroused by witnessing the unjust treatment of the Hebrew slave by the Egyptian guard. The moment it was done Musa ﷺ repented and was immediately forgiven. The white hand could not signify taking away the sin of unintentional manslaughter. This had been, anyway, already taken away. In addition it would not have been a sign that Pharaoh would have recognized or by which he would have been impressed.

In addition to the removal of any obvious physical scars, when he brought out his hand it shone with a visible light, which signified the Power given to him by Allah. In his right hand he held the authority to enact the Will of the Creator. Musa ﷺ was a law-giving prophet. In his right hand he was to carry the Law and the Word of Allah. As Allah says about those who repent and believe,

"Their light will run before them and on their right hands;" (66:8)

Allah was giving Musa ﷺ two signs, signs that could be used to convince his enemies that he was indeed a servant and a chosen Messenger of the Lord. One sign was the staff that could transform into fear. The second and more powerful of the signs was the hand that carried the light and could control the fear. Both the hand and the staff were ordinary, familiar, everyday objects that could transform in a most unordinary and extraordinary way. The ordinary physical reality, visible to the eye, had been replaced by a very extraordinary spiritual reality that had become also, suddenly and miraculously, visible to the eye. In just this way a seemingly drab and difficult life is transformed by its spiritual reality into something of great beauty and nobility. In the realm of Reality, the appearances of the world can be misleading. It is called a miracle when this Reality becomes visible in the everyday world.

Musa's ﷺ hand was strong and steady, used to hard work and even fighting. He put it to his heart and it became luminous, glowing even in broad daylight like the full moon. The staff of Musa ﷺ was fear that transformed into power. The hand of Musa ﷺ was power that transformed into light-giving Law. In the final revelation Allah tells the Prophet Muhammad ﷺ what he will see on the Day of Judgment:

"On that day you will see the believing men and the believing women, their light shining before them and on their right hands. Good news for you this day." (57:12)

This was the great sign. Musa's ﷺ right hand was already shining with light. He had taken off the shoes of this world. His humanity had been perfected and he had been dressed with the attributes of the heavens. He had been chosen and, while still in this life, he had been given the sign that he was of the people of Paradise.

$\dfrac{18}{48}$

19.

The Mission And The Message

Allah ordered Musa ﷺ to return to Egypt and do two things. First he must, with beautiful words and gentle manner, remind Pharaoh of his duty as the King of Egypt, "the shadow of God on earth", to be generous and just to God's creation. Pharaoh had crossed all boundaries of proper behavior and righteous conduct. He needed to be reminded of the favors he had received and his obligation to extend them to the people under his care. Second, for reasons of His own beyond our understanding, Allah had chosen the Banu Israil as the bearers of His covenant. Allah wanted Pharaoh to release them from slavery in Egypt and let them go with their Prophet wherever God directed them.

Allah did not admonish Pharaoh because of his disrespect for His Creator. Even though he was declaring himself to be a god this was not what was of concern to Allah. Whatever Pharaoh said or believed was of no consequence to the Almighty because it neither added to His Glory nor detracted from it. In the end it would only hurt Pharaoh himself. What aroused Divine retribution was that by considering himself to be a god Pharaoh acted without justice or mercy to the servants of Allah Almighty. This was the transgression for which Pharaoh was being held to account.

Allah commanded Musa ﷺ to undertake two, seemingly impossible, tasks. He must go to the mightiest king on the face of the earth at that time and admonish him for his tyranny and lack of respect for his Creator. In addition Musa ﷺ must demand the release of hundreds of thousands of Pharaoh's hardworking

His hand became luminous like the full moon.

slaves who were considered to be valuable property and assets of the state.

Musa ﷺ was thunderstruck. He did not question the need for Allah's commands. Nor did he doubt, even for a second, the possibility of their accomplishment. But many reasons came flooding into his mind about why he was not the one best equipped for the job and he began to list them desperately to his Lord. Musa ﷺ was, after all, not called "Kalimullah", the speaker with Allah, just because Allah spoke to him. He was given this title of honor because, out of all the prophets we know of, he was the only one who spoke back.

He said he would not find a warm welcome among the household of Pharaoh because he had in his youth preferred the company of their slaves. He had chosen the slave community of his origins over the aristocracy of his upbringing. He had rejected the favors of his adoptive family and chosen to align himself with the family of his birth.

He might have thought, as well, that he would not receive a warm welcome from the slave community either. He had, after all, been raised as a prince, among the enemies and persecutors of his people. He had fled Egypt many years before and was not well known among them. Why would the Banu Israil respond positively to his call? There was a good chance they would reject him and with him, the message of the Lord.

Then he was concerned that he had no ability as a public speaker. His chest tightened and he froze when placed in front of a crowd. Words did not come to him easily. Either he had a speech impediment, possibly caused by the burning coal of his childhood, or he spoke Egyptian or Hebrew with a heavy accent that was difficult to understand. Most probably he was a man of action rather than a man of words. He felt uneasy as a public speaker. He simply was not eloquent. As a young man he had traveled around the encampments of the Banu Israil with his brother, Harun ﷺ. He knew the difference between his ability to communicate and that of his brother and Musa ﷺ feared he would not be able to clearly deliver his Lord's message without assistance.

Finally he reminded his Creator that the people of Pharaoh wanted him for murder. He had been accused of a crime, the killing of an Egyptian guard. If he returned openly to Egypt they might arrest him and throw him into prison or even worse.

"He said: My Lord, I fear that they will reject me. And my breast straightens, and my tongue is not eloquent, so send for Harun. And they have a crime against me, so I fear they will kill me." (26:12-14)

His Lord was patient and understanding with him. Allah Almighty reassured His servant Musa ﷺ that he was surely protected. With his Lord's help he need fear no man. Both Pharaoh and the Banu Israil would receive him and not turn on him. He would find his tongue turned eloquent, his heart unwavering, and his voice firm. In case of overwhelming terror, Musa ﷺ was given a personal gift of reassurance. His most Merciful and Compassionate Lord, told him to pull his hand close to his side and he would find strength and confidence.

"And We make this [Quran] easy for your tongue so that you may bear good tidings with it to those who avoid evil" (19:97)

Allah Almighty spoke these words to His servant the Prophet Muhammad ﷺ several thousand years later. But all the Books of God must necessarily be imbued with the same blessings: They are incredibly beautiful, easy on the tongue and on the ear, and easy to remember.

"My Lord expand my breast for me: and ease my affair for me: and loose the knot from my tongue, so they may understand my speech. And give to me a helper from my family: Harun, my brother. Add to my strength by him, and make him share my task – so that we may glorify You much, and much remember You." (20:25-34)

And Allah answered,

> "You are indeed granted your request, O Musa." (20:36)
> "We shall strengthen your arm through your brother and grant you both authority so they will not reach you. With Our signs, you and those who follow you will be the victors." (28:35)

Then the Lord reminded Musa ﷺ of all the favors He had given to him in the past. From the moment of his conception his journey in the world had been prepared and guided. Allah Almighty had saved him from being killed by Pharaoh's soldiers at birth. He had inspired his mother to put him in the wooden box and set him adrift in the river. He had rescued him from the water and had him raised in the house of his enemies. He had returned him to his mother to be nursed. He forgave him and covered his tracks when he killed a man and fled from Egypt. He guided him through the wilderness and gave him protection in Madyan. And now He had brought him to the valley of Tuwa and into His Divine Presence. Allah had guided and protected him all of his life and He would not stop doing so now.

On Musa's ﷺ request his older brother Harun ﷺ was also confirmed as a prophet of God. The two brothers were authorized to act on behalf of their Maker and not to fear for they were promised success. They were commanded to go to the court of Pharaoh as emissaries from the one God, ambassadors from the Divine Kingdom.

> "Then come to Pharaoh and say, we are messengers from the Lord of the Worlds" (26:16)

This extraordinary encounter on the side of a mountain

in the wilderness of Sinai took place during three full days and nights. Some say it took seven days and nights. On each day Musa ﷺ bared his soul, asking one question or voicing one misgiving. Each day his Lord reassured him and counseled him, giving him more confidence and certainty. Strength upon strength, authority upon authority, until the Prophet Musa ﷺ was armed with signs and powers enough to face one of the strongest wielders of worldly authority who has ever lived. His days of peace and silence as an unknown shepherd, alone under the vast sky of his Lord's majestic creation, were abruptly over.

משה

19/48

20.

Return To Egypt

Musa ﷺ made his way back to where he had left his family many nights before. He leaned heavily on his staff as he walked. He did not carry a lighted coal or a burning branch and he did not have traveling directions or a map. He did, however, have the light of the Lord in his heart and a purpose for the future.

His family had been terribly worried for his safety. Saffura ؒ had given birth to another baby boy. She tried not to think that maybe her son had been born in the wilderness, an orphan. She feared the worst for her husband. Some of the men traveling with them had gone to look for Musa ﷺ and found no trace. They were herdsmen and trackers but they could find no footprints, nor any signs of their companion. The wild wind and storm had, by the Will of their Lord, erased all traces. Every day they went out, looking for Musa ﷺ but they neither heard nor saw anything.

The storm had subsided soon after Musa ﷺ had left. The next morning, Allah had made the sun to come out and warm the small family. They set up their tents and lit a big fire. Their belongings dried, and they got warm and cooked hot food. They decided to stay in that place to let the new mother recover before they traveled on, hoping beyond hope that their companion would return.

After many days they saw a figure approaching in the distance. Holding her breath, Saffura ؒ watched as the distant shape took form. Soon she recognized her dear husband and with relief and joy greeted him and showed him their new son.

They recognized each other by the light shining from their faces.

Musa ﷺ blessed the baby and named him Eliezer (God is help). After some days of resting and recuperating they packed up their tents and traveled on.

Some say that at the same time in Egypt, Harun ﷺ was blessed with the news that he had been chosen by Allah to be His prophet. He felt a great longing in his heart to see his brother and he was inspired to set out in the direction in which Musa ﷺ had fled so long ago. He met his brother halfway on the trail. They could recognize each other by the light shining from their faces. They shared their wonder at the awesome changes in their lives and the all-encompassing plan of Allah. They consulted on the best way to enter Egypt and approach Pharaoh.

Others say that Musa ﷺ traveled slowly with his family and animals, stopping to rest early each day and setting out again in the morning, until they reached Egypt. They went directly to the neighborhood where Imran ؓ and Yuchabad ؓ lived. There they asked permission to camp. Yuchabad ؓ and Mariam ؓ were the only ones at home so they did not actually go out to see the strangers. They gave their permission and welcomed the travelers from behind the door. Musa ﷺ and his family set up their tents and coralled their animals. Later that evening Yuchabad ؓ sent Mariam ؓ and Harun ﷺ with soup and bread for their guests.

Harun ﷺ stayed to eat with the family. After the meal they began to talk and tell the news. But, being polite, neither asked the other much about their origins or history. Ten years of heavy work in the heat of the sun had changed Musa ﷺ outwardly as well as inwardly. Neither Harun ﷺ nor Mariam ؓ recognized their brother. For three days Musa ﷺ accepted the hospitality of his father and mother. On the fourth day he revealed his true identity. We can only imagine with what joy and tears the family of Imran ؓ greeted the return of their beloved son.

Musa ﷺ was concerned that his older brother Harun ﷺ would not be pleased at his return. Harun ﷺ had had a very different life from that of Musa ﷺ. He was raised as a member of a low caste group under the total control of a king and a government, both unsympathetic and foreign in culture and language. Unlike his brother Musa ﷺ, Harun ﷺ had remained in the confines of his own group, being educated by his father, Imran ﷺ and the other elders of the Banu Israil in the ways of his people. They belonged to the tribe of Lavi which was the only tribe that kept the practices of Ibrahim ﷺ pure, and their belief in Allah strong.

As Harun ﷺ grew older he became a spokesman for his father and his people. He developed into an eloquent and inspiring speaker. He traveled throughout the villages and encampments of his people, teaching them, reminding them, supporting them. When needed he was the one to intercede between them and the government. He was the one who went to the palace to negotiate with Pharaoh on behalf of his people. He became skilled in diplomacy and was often successful in defending and protecting the Banu Israil against the savage and tyrannical aims of the government.

The people, in turn, had learned to respect Harun ﷺ. They looked up to him and they followed his advice. They began coming to him with all of their problems, domestic or financial. They knew him to be helpful in resolving disputes and reconciling differences. He became for them a peacemaker and an arbitrator. Harun ﷺ had married a girl of the Banu Israil named Elisheba, and they had had four sons together, Eleazer, Ithamar, Nadab, and Abihu.

It is said that Musa ﷺ felt hesitant to approach his brother when he first arrived in Egypt because he was afraid that Harun ﷺ would be jealous or resentful of either their different fortunes or their different gifts. He did not want to compete with Harun ﷺ for a position of power and respect among the peoples of Egypt. But Allah let him know that Harun ﷺ was not created with that kind of nature and when they met in Egypt Musa ﷺ could see that what Allah had said was true. Harun's ﷺ heart leapt with joy when he recognized Musa ﷺ. It did not occur to him to feel other than happiness at the good fortunes of his younger brother.

It is said that of all brothers, Musa ﷺ benefited his brother the most. When he was given his prophetic mission by Allah Almighty, he asked for additional help. At Musa's ﷺ request, his brother Harun ﷺ was also made a prophet of God and given divine authority. There was no jealousy or competition between the brothers, only goodwill and support.

The Bible says, "Behold how good and pleasant for brothers to dwell together in unity." (Psalms 133:1) And it says about their companionship, "Mercy and Truth are met; Righteousness and Peace have kissed." (Psalms 85:10) They were true brothers, walking side-by-side in the way of the Lord, one the helper of the other: one the ruler, one the priest. Harun ﷺ represented Mercy and Peace. Musa ﷺ represented Truth and Righteousness.

Even a prophet is a human being and needs the company of other men with enough understanding and knowledge to support him and give him good counsel and to keep him company when he stands alone against the darkness. The Prophet Muhammad ﷺ had his close companions including AbuBakr as-Siddiq ؓ and Ali Ibn AbiTalib ؓ. The Prophet Isa ﷺ had the twelve 'Hawariyyun,' his disciples. Musa ﷺ and Harun ﷺ had each other.

20/48

21.

Delivering The Message

Their first task was to get inside the palace to speak with Pharaoh. They had been told by Allah Almighty to invite Pharaoh kindly first, on the chance that the good in him was still strong enough to outweigh the bad. Allah has no desire to punish His creation. He always warns and provides many chances long before any punishment is meted out. We are always given the opportunity to correct ourselves and return to the right way before we are corrected and set straight against our will. Many of the prophets were sent to evildoing people to warn them and to offer them guidance to the right way. Lut ﷺ, Nuh ﷺ, Hud ﷺ, Salih ﷺ, Yunus ﷺ, to name a few, were all sent to warn their people that punishment was on its way if they did not return to the path of justice and mercy and stop abusing their power in the land.

Of these, only the people of Yunus ﷺ listened. After many years of preaching, Yunus ﷺ had the enormous satisfaction of seeing his people avoid punishment and come to safety. Just as the cloud of punishment approached their city the people of Yunus ﷺ accepted the sovereignty of God Almighty and submitted themselves to His Law. The threatened punishment was averted at the last minute and the people of Nineveh went on to live many years of good, righteous life.

The Prophet Muhammad ﷺ also had the joy of seeing his people accept the truth and believe in what was sent to them. But this only occurred after ten years of patient preaching while receiving only abuse and torture in return; followed by ten more years of political treachery and bloody warfare. Then and

"And if they were to see a fragment of the heaven falling, they would say: A heap of clouds." (52:44)

only then did the general community of the Prophet ﷺ finally relinquish the worthless customs and beliefs they had held so dear, and come to accept the life-giving faith that he was offering.

The story of the meeting between Musa ﷺ and Pharaoh is told in eight different chapters of the Quran. It is told with only some variation. Sometimes it is told as an example of what befalls the people who do not listen to the messengers that Allah sends and who do not heed His warnings. But sometimes the story is told, it seems, in order to reassure the Prophet Muhammad ﷺ, that things were also tough for other prophets. Their people were as unwilling to listen and as resistant to change. The story of Musa ﷺ serves as an example of the arrogant, outrageous nature of mankind and of the patient kindness with which Allah Almighty attempts to bring them into line with truth.

Musa ﷺ and Harun ﷺ decided on a direct course of action. They went together to seek an audience with Pharaoh at his palace. They approached in the accepted manner. They went up to the gate and asked to see the king and then they waited to be given an answer. It is clear that getting an audience with the Pharaoh was not an easily or quickly achieved task. By some accounts they stood outside the gates for two years before Pharaoh was even told that they were asking to see him. This gives some indication of how removed Pharaoh was from his own people. He was no longer accessible. He no longer was even aware of the needs of his people nor concerned to listen to their requests.

The palace is described as consisting of many concentric walls; the outer walls were guarded by soldiers, while the inner walls were guarded by lions and other hungry beasts. It was a labyrinth, requiring patience and fearlessness. Whether this is a description of the actual construction of the palace walls or the effect created by layers of bureaucracy and a maze of political functionaries, either way the walls were not easily breached.

It took a long time and much patience before the two brothers stood before the Pharaoh. They entered where he sat on his golden throne, draped in gold and beads, his face painted, his beard manicured and oiled. He looked more like a statue than a man of flesh and blood. He was surrounded on all sides by courtiers, who competed with each other to please him. There was hardly an honest face among them. Imagine two men coming out of the desert to stand before the most powerful man on earth, emissaries from the Kingdom of Heaven to the earthy kingdom.

The Prophets stood before the court, tall and straight. Their beards were left long and were turning grey, for Musa ﷺ was now maybe forty years old and Harun ﷺ three years his senior. They wore the ankle length wool robes of the Hebrew shepherd rather than the short linen waistcloth of the aristocratic Egyptian. They carried tall staffs in their hands and their heads were wrapped in tiers of turban cloth. They had no rich clothes, no necklaces of gold nor medallions of silver. Their honors had been bestowed on them by the Highest King, and it showed as light on their faces and sincerity in their eyes.

In spite of the changes, Pharaoh immediately recognized his foster son, Musa ﷺ, more quickly than his own mother had recognized him. Pharaoh was surprised at his return and asked him his purpose. Musa ﷺ answered him, straight to the point, without any guile,

"Indeed, we are messengers of the Lord of all the worlds; Send with us the Children of Israil." (26:16)

Pharaoh was shocked and a little amused at the daring of this renegade son, to return openly and confront him and then ask for an enormous favor. He immediately reminded Musa ﷺ of the favors already bestowed on him, of the fact that he had been a foundling, dredged out of the river Nile and adopted and raised with the best of everything. Nothing had been denied him. Pharaoh tried to make him feel guilt or a sense of indebtedness. He played with the words of his estranged son. Musa ﷺ said he was a messenger of the Lord, literally, of the one who loves and cherishes. Pharaoh twisted this word and turned it back on him. He said,

"Did we not cherish you among ourselves as a child, and you stayed with us for years of your life?" (26:18)

Pharaoh is implying that he is Musa's ﷺ lord and cherisher. He reminds Musa ﷺ of the favors he gave him just as Allah Almighty, in the valley of Tuwa, reminded Musa ﷺ of His favors. But Allah reminded him in order to calm his heart and make him feel secure, to reassure him that he had always been protected and cared for. Pharaoh reminded Musa ﷺ in order to try to belittle him and make him feel indebted and ashamed.

Then Pharaoh reminded him threateningly of the terrible tragedy, the killing of the guard, which had ended Musa's ﷺ adoptive life and sent him alone into the wilderness, hunted and accused, homeless and destitute. This was the very same tragedy by which Allah Almighty chose to favor him, by stripping him of the things of this temporary world so that He could bestow on him the goods of eternity.

Pharaoh accused Musa ﷺ of killing one of his officers and betraying him. Musa ﷺ chose the Banu Israil above his Egyptian adopted family. He chose to defend the rights of the downtrodden over those of the masters among whom he had been raised. He did not need the forgiveness or understanding of Pharaoh. He had repented and been forgiven by Allah. He had stood up against oppression and in the process had, without intending to, killed a man. Now he intended to complete the action he had begun, by standing up for, and freeing, all of Israil. This time he acted with God's hand above his hand. Injustice stood no chance.

"I did it, then, when I was among the erring. So I fled from you when I feared you, but my Lord granted me wisdom and made me among the messengers." (26:20-21)

The murder was an action committed when his

understanding was incomplete. He had been impetuous and acted before he had received authority from God to act. If he was misguided it was only in this way. If you act on your own you will have to face the consequences on your own. If you act with God's authority He will protect you and shelter you. Musa ﷺ acted on his own and so paid the price. At that time he still feared men and their laws. Now he had returned as a Prophet of God and feared nothing and no one, but God. Now he knew Whom he served and Who his master truly was.

He proceeded to answer Pharaoh's implication that he owed him a favor for the kindness shown him in his youth; that he owed Pharaoh the respect and deference of a child to a father. He said,

"And this is the favor of which you remind me: that you have enslaved the Children of Israil?" (26:22)

Pharaoh clearly had done no real favor for Musa ﷺ. It was Pharaoh's own actions that had created the chain of events that had led up to their confrontation. By enslaving, mistreating and torturing the Banu Israil, Pharaoh had created the very reason for the abandonment of the baby Musa ﷺ, the need for his adoption by strangers, and in the end, for the killing of the guard in order to stop the oppression of the weak.

Pharaoh had done all in his power to avoid destiny. As Jalaluddin Rumi (q) says about Pharaoh in the "Mathnawi", "Within his (Pharaoh's) house was Musa safe and sound, while he was killing babes outside to no purpose." But a man cannot outwit his Creator. Pharaoh had killed all those innocent Hebrew babies in order to eliminate the one, and that one Allah caused Pharaoh to rescue with his own hand from a watery grave, and place in the warmth of his own house, to raise to manhood. Destiny cannot be altered, only the way in which it is greeted.

Musa ﷺ faced Pharaoh, straight and sure. Pharaoh could find no weakness or faltering. This, of course, made him even angrier. He called his ministers, his court, his palace guards, and even his servants, to witness that this ingrate son was denying his lordship, refusing to worship him and even claiming another God in his place. In addition Musa ﷺ claimed to be the spokesman of that unseen God and so was placing himself in direct opposition to Pharaoh.

All the while Musa ﷺ continued to call Pharaoh to come back to the Lord; to return to the God he already knew, to return to the Truth he already recognized. Pharaoh deceitfully pretended to be ignorant of this fact. He asked Musa ﷺ about the God on whose behalf he spoke. Musa ﷺ answered that Pharaoh already knew quite well who He was.

"Your Lord and the Lord of your ancestors." (26:26)

Musa ﷺ reminded Pharaoh that his ancestors had not declared themselves to be gods as he did. They knew the one God, the Creator and Sustainer of the world. Clearly Musa ﷺ expected his words to strike a chord in Pharaoh's heart. He warned him that the Lord had sent him in order to give Pharaoh a chance to reform, to be just, to be penitent, to be humble and merciful: to let the Children of Israel go free.

A Sign For Pharaoh

The concept of a single God threw into question the foundation upon which Pharaoh's power depended. He turned to face Musa ﷺ and threatened him that if he persisted in worshipping a god other than Pharaoh he would be arrested for treason and either killed or imprisoned. But Musa ﷺ was sure in his knowledge of the promise his Lord had given him on the mountain. Allah would let no one harm His servant. Pharaoh laughed and thought that he had Musa ﷺ cornered. In front of all his court he planned to ridicule and discredit him. He asked Musa ﷺ to show a sign that would prove beyond doubt, that his God really existed and that he was His messenger.

Musa ﷺ threw down his staff as he had been instructed. It transformed immediately into an enormous serpent, spitting fire and smoke, lashing its tail, its eyes red with fire. The men assembled in the throne room fled to the outer edges looking for shelter. The Pharaoh toppled off his throne and crawled under it quickly to hide. But the dragon had spotted him. It turned and fixed its fiery eyes upon him. It leapt forward, clearly intending to swallow the whole throne in its poisonous mouth. It gnashed it fangs, making a ghastly grating sound so that all those hearing shuddered and grimaced with horror. From under his golden throne the voice of Pharaoh could be heard imploring Musa ﷺ to call off his dragon. In his fear he agreed to comply with any and all requests Musa ﷺ might make. He promised, with all his court as witnesses, that he would let the Children of Israil go with Musa ﷺ, go with all their belongings and never come back.

It leapt forward clearly intending to swallow the whole throne.

Musa ﷺ stretched out his hand and grabbed the dragon by its jaw, just before it reached the throne. Instantly it transformed back into a harmless stick, carved from the branch of a tree such as any shepherd might carry. Pharaoh pulled himself to his feet quickly before most of the court had returned from where they had taken shelter. Little by little, the men returned to the throne room, shaken and laughing nervously. What had they seen? Was it a miracle or was it a magic trick? Most of them decided it was trickery but that these shepherds were better magicians than any they had ever seen before. Magic was well known in Egypt and the court officials were too cosmopolitan to be impressed or moved by a magician's tricks, however good.

This is not a unique response to the appearance of miracles. The Prophet Muhammad ﷺ was asked to perform a miracle. With his Lord's permission, the full moon split into two parts, separated and appeared to pass through the sleeves of his robe before uniting again in its usual place in the sky. The Quraysh, inconceivably, were not impressed and dismissed the miracle as a magician's trick. The Prophet Isa ﷺ was asked to bring food down from the heavens to feed a crowd of people. Before he asked his Lord to make this miracle happen, he warned the people that disbelief would no longer be accepted after the display of a miracle. If Allah bends the laws of nature to make a reality from the spiritual world apparent in the material world, then to refuse to believe your eyes is no longer an acceptable excuse. Even so, in every age, men refuse to believe in miracles. In The Quran it says

"And if they were to see a fragment of the heaven falling, they would say: A heap of clouds." (52:44)

There were many reasons that up to this point Pharaoh thought of himself as godlike. He never experienced sickness or ill health of any kind. He was very old, much older than most other people and still strong and clear-headed. He held enormous wealth, and the power of life and death over much of the known world. These, of course, were favors from Allah Almighty for which Pharaoh should have been thankful rather than proud. He had begun to think he was deserving of these grants and no one in his court gave him any advice to the contrary.

Another reason that Pharaoh thought himself like a god rather than a mortal human was that for years he had needed to use the toilet only once in forty days. After this incident with the dragon of Musa ﷺ Pharaoh was so rattled and afraid that, to his humiliation, he found himself having to use the toilet forty times in only one day.

When the court had reassembled, Musa ﷺ put his hand inside his robe and brought it out shining like the moon. Its radiance lit up the room, poured through the open doors and windows, bounced off the lofty ceiling and forced the onlookers to shield their eyes. The already rattled courtiers gasped with astonishment. This was a trick they had never seen before and they peered up at their master, the Pharaoh, hoping that he would show them the appropriate response. But Pharaoh was concerned with only one thing - to hide his weakness in front of his people. He applauded as if enjoying a good show and, yawning loudly, turned to leave the room. Rushing to the toilet he whispered over his shoulder to Musa ﷺ that he should return later and they would talk privately.

For in actuality, Pharaoh was very impressed. He had seen many things in his long life and met all kinds of people. What he witnessed this night was different from all of that and it had him thinking about possibilities he had long forgotten. When Musa ﷺ and Harun ﷺ returned they felt that there might be an opening in Pharaoh's heart. They pleaded with him to listen to their words and to accept the invitation of the Lord of the Worlds.

They patiently explained the reality that we are all servants of the one true Master, the Creator of all that exists. We have no function other than to obey Him and to be helpful and generous to His creation. Pharaoh listened and asked what would be his reward if he accepted what was being offered him. He was told that if he accepted to worship Allah, Musa ﷺ would ask that he be given youth that does not age, dominion that does not decline, health uninterrupted by sickness, and paradise for eternity. Even to Pharaoh this sounded like an offer too good to refuse. He asked for time to consult his advisors.

To consult with others is one the requirements of a believer. The Prophet Muhammad ﷺ said that religion is good advice. Before making an important decision it is necessary to take good and honest counsel. If there is no one appropriate around with whom to consult, then consult your self. Whatever your self advises, be suspicious of its motives, be wary, be cautious and then, do the opposite. Since all religion speaks from the same Truth, Musa ﷺ respected the Pharaoh's request and left him time to seek the advice of his counselors.

Pharaoh immediately betook himself to the apartments of his beloved wife Asiya ﷺ. He told her his dilemma. However, he omitted to tell her who had posed it, for he knew her love for the Hebrew foundling they had pulled out of the river so long ago. He knew the sadness that had descended on her heart when her son Musa ﷺ had fled and never returned. He didn't want to tell her that it had been he who had put a price on her son's head, and that for fear of him, Musa ﷺ had fled into the wilderness. He didn't want to tell her that this renegade son had returned, not as their son but as a son of Israil; not serving Pharaoh but serving another mightier God; not humbly asking forgiveness but proudly giving commands. Instead Pharaoh did tell Asiya ؓ that a madman had entered the palace and had offered him a marvelous reward if he would just believe in Allah and worship only Him.

Asiya ؓ was one who was truly guided without benefit of a teacher. She heard what her husband told her and she recognized that it was not the offer of a madman but it was the truth. Quickly but carefully she advised him to accept this most generous offer; to believe in God and become the recipient of the greatest rewards. Pharaoh left her apartments bent on accepting Musa's offer. But in the hallway he met his chief counselor, Haman. Haman counseled for the devil. Haman said, "You who are master of everything, would you now become the servant of another? You can continue to look young by dying your hair and beard. The army and the police keep the kingdom secure in your grasp. Your health is guaranteed under the care of your most expensive physicians. And, as for Paradise, it already exists in the gardens of your kingdom."

Almost did Pharaoh turn in the right direction. Almost did the gentle words of Musa ﷺ convince the old king to reform his ways. But that was not to be. Instead Pharaoh bent to the flattery of Haman and sought counsel with his advisors on how to defeat and discredit the two brothers who had dared to offer him Eternity.

משה

22/48

Dragon Magic

Pharaoh's advisors suggested that he call all the magicians of Egypt and its provinces, to come to a competition. The winner would be granted a huge reward as well as closeness to the king. Egypt at that time concentrated all its scholarly efforts on science and discovery. There were more magicians in that land than in any other before or since and they were skilled and powerful. They were men of learning who used their knowledge of chemistry and physics, astronomy and natural science, to fool and entertain the people. They were educated men who used their knowledge to gain power and wealth and to manipulate the people in service to the state. They were also like the scientists of their time.

Pharaoh was confident that his magicians would prevail. He was so sure that he scornfully offered Musa ﷺ and Harun ﷺ the choice of the date and place of the competition. Musa ﷺ chose the day of the great festival when all the people would be assembled. He and Harun ﷺ would have an opportunity to speak before the largest crowd and to demonstrate the power of their Lord. It was to be a public competition in which the people could choose between truth and falsehood.

The day arrived and the field designated for the competition filled with thousands of the curious. There were so many spectators that even the hills were studded with people who had packed their lunches and brought their children. Some even watched from small boats, floating on the nearby river. Fifteen thousand magicians arrived on the appointed day. Among them seventy-two master magicians appeared, to take

The dragon scooped up in its terrible jaws each of the magicians' contrivances.

up the challenge. They stood at one end of the field dressed in outfits of splendor; bright colors studded with jewels and gold, fashions from the exotic places where they had studied. On the other side of the field they were faced by two bearded men in the plain, undyed, woolen robes of slaves.

Musa ﷺ and Harun ﷺ by command of Allah Almighty had come to compete with the best sorcerers in the world. They stood by themselves, facing the array of confident deceivers. Musa ﷺ held firmly the staff of Adam ﷺ in his right hand as he gazed out over the field swarming with spectators. He felt shy and a little anxious as he wondered how they would be able to represent the Almighty against these men of science. But Allah spoke to them and steadied their hearts.

The magicians, on their side, were also taken aback by the simple and honest appearance of their competitors. They did not look at all like magicians, or sorcerers, or men skilled at deception. They looked like righteous men, simple and straightforward. As a consequence, the magicians also became uneasy and wondered what this competition was really about. Were they being led into some sort of trap? They could not help but defer to, and show respect for, their honorable looking opponents. They asked them who should be the first to perform.

Allah inspired Musa ﷺ to tell the magicians to go first. So the magicians spread themselves in a line across the field, facing his majesty the Pharaoh. Each one threw his stick, or his rope, or his staff. By trickery and magic, by chemicals and strings, the sticks bent and wriggled and moved on the field as if they were living snakes.

Musa ﷺ and Harun ﷺ looked on in shame. How could the people see this trickery, this foolishness, and believe in it. How could they show the people clearly the difference between the power to actually create, which they represented, and the cheap power to deceive, which opposed them?

"So Musa ﷺ conceived a fear in his mind. We said, Fear not, surely you are the uppermost. And cast down what is in your right hand – it will eat up what they have made. What they have made is only the trick of an enchanter, and the enchanter succeeds not wherever he comes from." (20:67-69)

Musa ﷺ threw his staff to the ground. It became the fearsome dragon, breathing fire and smoke, thrashing its stupendous tail and gnashing its horrible teeth. The spectators drew back in fear. The ones closest to the frightening scene turned to run. It is said that thousands of people were crushed to death in the stampeding crowd. The dragon scooped up in its terrible jaws each and every one of the magicians' awkward contrivances and sucked them into its long scaly belly. Then the dragon turned its fiery eye on the Pharaoh and the dignitaries sitting with him. Moving with great speed, Musa ﷺ had just enough time to reach out and grab the dragon by the tip of its terrible tail. In an instant there was quiet and calm. All that remained of the great dragon was the simple staff lying inert in the right hand of the Prophet of God ﷺ.

The sticks, the ropes, the cords of the seventy-two magicians were nowhere to be found. The magicians looked for their precious implements and found no trace of any of them anywhere. Then they knew their opponents were no magicians. There was no trick or treachery here. If it had been an apparition then when the dragon disappeared their sticks and cords would have reappeared. This had been an extraordinary manifestation, a real miracle, the truth from a Truthful God. They understood trickery and so conversely, this made them able to recognize truth. What they had just witnessed was certainly truth. Without hesitation, convinced beyond the shadow of a doubt, all seventy-two magicians bowed down before the two servants of the Lord and prayed for forgiveness.

"We believe in the Lord of the Worlds, the Lord of Musa and Harun." (7: 121-122)

If Allah Almighty can transform the dead branch of a

tree into a vehicle for Truth then what is He able to do with the heart of a man?

23/48

24.

A House In Paradise

The Pharaoh was furious. Not only had all the magicians failed to discredit and defeat Musa ﷺ and Harun ﷺ but they had accepted their God in front of the assembled crowd. They had bowed down to their Creator, without even thinking about, or acknowledging Pharaoh himself who was sitting just above them on the podium. This was treason. This was treachery. It would only appear to be weakness if he showed any mercy. Pharaoh condemned all seventy-two magicians to death on the spot, without trial or recourse.

"He [Pharaoh] said, "Have you believed in him before I gave you leave? Surely, he is the chief of you, the same that taught you magic. I shall assuredly cut off your hands and feet alternately, then I shall crucify you upon the trunks of palm-trees; you shall know for certain which of us is more terrible in punishment and more lasting." (20:71)

The magicians did not flinch or try to retract their words. At the opening of the contest, impressed by the noble appearance of their competitors, they had shown respect to Allah's servants by inviting Musa ﷺ and Harun ﷺ to go first. Because of this small act Allah had leaned towards these men of learning and opened their hearts to accept faith. They had seen the truth and its light filled their hearts and minds and they would never accept to go back into the darkness. They submitted to the Will of their Lord and to the punishment of the Pharaoh. These men whose lives were based on deceit, embraced the truth and

"My Lord build for me a house in Paradise near You" (66:11)

knew its value. Better to die than to live and deny the truth they had witnessed. They traded a short life in this world of trials for an eternity of closeness to God in paradise. They answered Pharaoh:

"Never will we prefer you to what has come to us of clear proofs and over Him Who created us. Therefore, decree whatever you will decree. You can decree only concerning this worldly life. Indeed, we have believed in our Lord, that He may forgive us our sins and that which you compelled us to of magic. And God is best and most enduring." (20:72-73)

Because of these lines in The Hoy Quran some have said that forty of the seventy-two magicians had not chosen this occupation on their own. Rather, they had been children of the Banu Israil who had been forced to apprentice to the magicians. They had been born believers and they remembered their faith. Now they freely expressed what was always in their hearts. But God knows best.

Some say that Musa ﷺ prayed for them and so they were able, somehow, to escape Pharaoh's punishment and be hidden among the community of believers. But most chroniclers agree that these seventy-two magicians and sorcerers were shown the highest of God's favors, by converting and dying as martyrs on the very same day. At sunrise they had gotten out of bed, magicians and unbelievers. By the time that same sun had set, they had died martyrs and the most honored of believers.

Asiya ؑ sat beside her husband and watched the whole drama unfold. She saw her son, the beautiful boy she had pulled from the river, had educated and loved. She saw that he had grown powerful and straight, that light shone around him and from every limb of his body. She heard him speak carefully and with strength, when she knew how difficult this was for him, and how shy he had used to be. She felt pride for him and great respect and she listened carefully to every word he spoke. She felt no fear when the dragon lashed his tail at the crowd. She did not dive under her seat when the sparks flew in her direction. She stood on her feet, her eyes fixed on this glorious son of hers and her heart soared.

She watched the magicians accept the truth and submit. In her heart she submitted with them. When her husband the Pharaoh condemned them to death she rose to her feet and tried to plead for their lives. But Pharaoh was beyond reasoning with. He had been shamed before his court and his people. His anger knew no bounds. Now he turned on Asiya ؇ and blamed the whole affair on her. She had been the one to rescue the baby who was now responsible for this disaster. She had counseled him to accept the terms Musa ؇ had offered. Was she one of them, a traitor and a betrayer? Pharaoh threatened her also saying, "You wanted me to accept Musa's ؇ promise of paradise, now take it yourself." Asiya ؇ raised her hands to her Lord and asked with all her heart,

"My Lord! Build for me a house in Paradise near You, and deliver me from Pharaoh and his work, and deliver me from evil-doing people." (66:11)

And Allah Almighty accepted her prayer.

Musa ؇ could do nothing but watch as the Egyptian guards took the magicians and martyred them in horrible ways. They were torn limb from limb and then they were hung on palm trees to die. But not one of them changed his mind or asked to be spared. Not one of them pleaded or complained or even so much as sighed. The light of their new faith shone from their eyes and strengthened their hearts so that they did not feel the pain.

Pharaoh's love for his queen prevented him from following through on his threats. Asiya ؇ continued to live in the palace and to enjoy his affection. But after this incident she must have secretly made contact with her long lost son. He told her all that had been told to him and taught her how to worship God and how to glorify Him. What she heard she realized she already knew and believed. She became a devoted follower of Musa ﷺ without hesitation or reservation. Back in the palace she shared her convictions and faith with those close to her.

One day one of the Queen's ladies-in-waiting dropped a comb in the presence of Pharaoh. She stooped to pick it up and was heard to utter the words, Bismi Allahi r-Rahmani r-Rahim. "What is this? Who is this Allah? Who taught you these words?" shouted Pharaoh and he began to question her with intensity. She did not reveal that it was the Queen herself who had taught her these words. But neither would she take them back nor would she accept Pharaoh as her god and lord. So she and her husband, who was a minister of the treasury, together with their five children were condemned to death by being boiled alive.

Even to save the lives of her children this servant of Allah would not deny His Lordship. She might have wavered, however, when they tore her nursing baby from her arms but Allah strengthened her heart by making her infant son speak so the whole court could hear. In a baby voice that rose clearly over the bubbling water and the steam, he told her of the angels who were reaching out to comfort him and the gardens of paradise within his sight. Then she gladly followed her whole family in death. Her only request was to be buried together with them in one grave.

According to Hadith, the Prophet Muhammad ﷺ, while riding the Buraq from Mecca to Jerusalem on the Night Journey, smelled a beautiful perfume coming from the vicinity of Egypt. When he asked what it was, the Archangel Jibrail ﷺ told him that the angels had built a paradise garden within the grave of this loyal lady and her family. They will continue to live in that garden until they are admitted to the Gardens of Paradise on the Day of Judgment. It was the fragrance of its flowers that the Prophet ﷺ could smell.

Asiya ﷺ could not bear to hear the news of her loyal friend's death. She went to her husband, the Pharaoh, and accused him of murder, injustice and cruelty. Pharaoh could no longer excuse his Queen. In front of the whole court she had laid bare her treachery, her deceit. She had publicly declared that Pharaoh was not a god and that he was human and made terrible mistakes. Pharaoh asked his wife to take back her statements. But Asiya ﷺ had had enough and she would not back down. She declared: there is no god but the One God, the God of Musa ﷺ and Harun ﷺ. Pharaoh turned his back on her and sentenced her also to die a most horrible death.

The story of Asiya's ﷺ death is related to us from the eminent companions of the Prophet ﷺ, and recorded in the Hadith. First he had her hung on a palm tree under the relentless Egyptian sun. Every day he visited her and asked her to take back her words and return with him to the palace. She would not change her mind for all the wealth and luxury of Egypt. So he had her whipped. She would neither cry out nor renounce her faith. Then he denied her water. But her heart remained whole and never did she even consider denying her belief or asking for mercy from her torturers. But Musa ﷺ, her son, did ask for mercy for her from his Lord. Allah displayed before her eyes the mansion in Paradise waiting for her arrival, close to His Divine Presence in the highest heaven. Her suffering became sweetness then and her eyes saw only joy.

It is said that after the Day of Judgment Asiya ﷺ the Queen will be honored by being one of the brides of the Prophet Muhammad ﷺ for the rest of eternity. She is mentioned in the Quran (66:11) together with Maryam ﷺ, the mother of the Prophet Isa ﷺ, as the two highest examples of believing women. In addition there is a Hadith of the Prophet Muhammad ﷺ in which he is reported to have said: "There are many among men who have attained to perfection but among women none, except Maryam ﷺ, the mother of Isa ﷺ, and Asiya ﷺ, the wife of Pharaoh." May Allah bless them and continue to raise them closer.

משה

24/48

25.

For Whom The River Stops

For the next forty years Allah kept His prophets in Egypt. Their apparent task was twofold. They were to try to persuade Pharaoh to return to the worship of God and to try to negotiate the freedom of the Banu Israil. But they were also trying to establish and organize, from among the Banu Israil as well as from the general population, a community of believers firm in their worship and knowledge of God. The events described in the following chapters took place within that time period but there are differences of opinion as to the exact chronology and sequence. Only Allah knows the truth. So read the following stories and think of them as being threads that are interwoven to form the tapestry that was Musa's ﷺ sojourn in Egypt as a prophet.

Every day for the next forty years Musa ﷺ and Harun ﷺ returned to Pharaoh's palace. They would take turns standing by the great gate, waiting patiently for an opening. They spoke to whoever would listen and gave advice and help to whoever was seeking it. They observed the politics and daily running of the state. Their shining faces became an accepted part of the everyday life at the court of Pharaoh, while they waited for God to open the hearts of the Egyptians. And always, whenever an opportunity presented itself, they spoke gently and persuasively to Pharaoh himself. He saw them every day, as he came and went for pleasure or for matters of state.

One day Pharaoh stopped on his way into the palace. He saw Musa ﷺ standing as usual by the gate and he had an idea that he hoped would put an end to the conflict once and

The Merciful God heard His servant's prayer and stopped the river's flow.

for all. He offered a contest to see which of their gods was the true one. Pharaoh suggested that the next day the two of them should meet on the banks of the River Nile and command it, in the name of each of their gods, to stop flowing. Whichever one the river obeyed was the one whose god was most powerful.

That night Musa ﷺ went back to his house and prayed. He prayed the prayer of the evening and the prayer of the night. He slept a little then got up to praise and remember God as he did in the dark of every night. At the end he asked for Divine support in the contest that would take place the next morning. Then Musa ﷺ lay down and went confidently to sleep.

Pharaoh, however, went back to his palace. He dismissed his servants. He shut the ebony shutters and locked the golden doors. He lit one small candle that flickered over the beautiful paintings of the birds and flowers of Egypt that decorated his walls. He did not lie down upon his ivory bed or lay his head upon his downy pillow. Instead he climbed on an inlaid table and removed the chandelier that hung from a large hook in the ceiling. He tied a tight knot in his beard and hung himself by his beard from the hook. Then, with his feet dangling in air, he began to speak to God. "O Allah, " he said, "You are the One Almighty God, before Whom I am nothing. I beg You, do not shame me before all my people tomorrow. I beg You, just this one time, to hear my prayer and make me victorious tomorrow. After that You can do with me whatever You will."

Pharaoh hung like this, tears steaming down his cheeks from the pain, all night long. For the sin of pulling his precious beard so long ago, he would have killed the child Musa ﷺ. Now, still for the purpose of defeating Musa ﷺ, he was pulling out the precious hairs of his own beard.

Towards morning, when Pharaoh was too tired and dizzy to be thinking clearly, he saw a young man enter his locked bedroom. He could not be sure if he was dreaming or waking and he was helpless to do anything, so he pretended that everything was perfectly normal.

"O Pharaoh" the man said. "I have an urgent problem

for which I need your advice. I have a servant. I loved him dearly and trusted him and gave him every privilege and power. Now I have found out that he abused my gifts. He kept everything for himself. He beat my other servants. He gave orders under my name that were unknown to me and he did not carry out the orders with which I entrusted him. What can I do about this man?"

"Ah" said Pharaoh, hanging by his beard and not able to speak very clearly. "Either sentence him to burning or drown him. That should be the appropriate punishment."

"Will you put your name to this legal judgment?" asked the man. And Pharaoh, with great difficulty, drew the hieroglyphic of his name on the papyrus the man held out to him.

When the sun finally rose, Pharaoh untied his beard from the hook and fell in a heap on the floor. He lay there in some pain for a while and then slowly got up and got himself ready. He dressed in his royal robes of crimson and purple. He combed and oiled his very sore chin and put the tall crown of the two Egypts upon his head. He went out, with trepidation, to meet Musa ﷺ by the banks of the River Nile.

Musa ﷺ had risen early also and was waiting for Pharaoh. He wore as always his shepherd's coat of wool and he carried his staff in his right hand. His brother Harun ﷺ stood beside him. The banks of the river were packed with spectators anxious to see for themselves what the outcome of this contest would be.

Pharaoh with unaccustomed deference allowed the Prophet Musa ﷺ the first try. Musa ﷺ raised his staff and commanded the river, in the name of its Almighty Lord, to cease flowing. All eyes were fixed on the running water before them. Some thought they saw the water pause, some thought they saw the current turn backwards. But after some moments they agreed that they saw no change at all.

Pharaoh then stepped forward and, with all his heart, begged the river, in the name of the Almighty God, to stop its flow. The Merciful God, the Answerer of Prayers, heard His servant Pharaoh, and He stopped the mighty Nile from flowing.

It is clear that Pharaoh knew very well whom to ask and where to turn when he was truly in need. He knew who really held the power of life and death. That day Pharaoh thought he had won a decisive victory. That day he had in fact signed his own death sentence because he was the servant who had betrayed the trust of his master, Allah Almighty. And that day Musa ﷺ also was made to bear a very heavy test; for no one of the people knew that both men had prayed in the name of the same God and that God, the only God, the Most Merciful, had answered the most pitiful and weakest of the two.

$$\frac{25}{48}$$

26.

Nine Warning Signs

During the forty years in Egypt, while the prophets tried to remain patient and generous, God sent a series of obvious signs for the purpose of warning Pharaoh and his men that eventually there would come an end to patience. There were terrible consequences waiting for Pharaoh and his men at the end of the path they were walking. As much as Allah offered them goodness and success for obedience and righteousness, He also warned them of the consequences in punishment and destruction if they did not listen and change their ways.

Before He punishes or destroys a nation, Allah always sends clear signs and messengers to warn the people. He reminds them of the purpose of their creation and outlines for them the path to happiness and success. He says,

"And we destroyed no township but it had its warners." (26:208)

In this case, first Allah sent a drought. The rains did not fall. The river did not swell and flood the fields. In normal years the Nile would flood its banks and deposit fertile mud washed down from mountains many hundreds of miles to the south. This black soil was easy to work and easy to plant. The crops grew in abundance, enough for the farmers, for the cities, and to be sold abroad. Egypt grew most of the wheat and barley eaten in the whole Middle East.

For three years no rain fell. The crops dwindled, sickened

"There were nine signs sent to Pharaoh and his folk." (27:12)

and died. There was nothing to sell abroad. Then there was nothing to sell in the city markets. Finally there was nothing to eat at home. The people consulted their priests and their gods to no avail then they begged Pharaoh to talk to Musa ﷺ. Pharaoh promised that if Musa ﷺ asked his Lord to relieve the drought, Pharaoh would believe in the One God and he would let the Children of Israil go free.

So Musa ﷺ prayed to his Lord to release the rain and to put an end to the famine. Allah the Most Generous, opened the clouds of Heaven and it began to rain. For a few days Pharaoh and his people rejoiced, but then they began to mutter that this was only a natural occurrence. Droughts had happened before and they had ended eventually in rain. So Pharaoh felt no obligation to keep his promise. He did not liberate the Children of Israil and he did not bow down to his Creator. This is the nature of man. When he is in trouble or sickness he prays sincerely but as soon as he is well or his circumstances improve, he loses interest and puts his Lord out of his mind.

So the rains kept coming, soaking the countryside and soaking the cities. The roads washed away, the fields became basins of soft mud. There was no path on which to walk and no road on which to drive to market. The seeds they so painstakingly planted just floated away in the rivers of mud. The roofs of the houses became saturated with water and collapsed. The temples and pyramids became waterfalls. The storehouses flooded. The people again beseeched their Pharaoh to make a deal with Musa ﷺ.

Once again Pharaoh approached Musa ﷺ and made an offer to believe in the one God and to let the Children of Israil go free, if only Musa ﷺ would implore his Lord to end the rain. Musa ﷺ opened his hands and asked Allah Almighty to put an end to the rain. The skies cleared. The sun appeared. Egypt began to dry out. Pharaoh relaxed; rains had come and gone before. Once more he ignored his promises. The farmers planted their seeds and watched them grow. The plants were stronger and taller than ever before. The seed heads were bursting and so heavy that their stems were as thick as trees in order to support the weight.

One morning the Egyptians woke to the sound of a strange buzzing. Looking out of their houses they saw a dark cloud on the horizon. As they watched, it came closer and closer until suddenly, it was upon them. It was a cloud of locusts – ravenous grasshoppers that devoured everything in sight. They ate the crops in the fields until there was not one blade standing. They ate the straw roofs off the houses. They ate the clothes drying on the lines. They ate the wooden doors and window frames. Some claim they even ate the iron hinges that had held the doors in place. They ate, and they ate, until the people were afraid that they themselves would be the next victims.

Again they ran to Pharaoh and made him promise Musa ﷺ whatever he wanted, if he would only beg his Lord to remove the locusts. Once more Pharaoh promised. Once more Musa ﷺ gave him the benefit of the doubt, and prayed to his Lord. The cloud of locusts passed out of Egypt; they had eaten everything there was to eat anyway. The obdurate people muttered that locusts had come and gone before.

Life returned to normal and the Children of Israil waited. But Pharaoh did not keep his promise. To no one's surprise he continued on exactly as he had before. The next sign Allah inflicted on the obstinate, unfaithful Egypt was the worst so far. In every house, in every corner, in every field, on every blade of grass Allah caused insects to hatch. There were bugs everywhere; beetles in the beds, centipedes in the water, flies in the food. When they walked they squashed cockroaches between their toes. They were afraid to sit or lie down for fear of where the bugs might crawl. When they breathed, they inhaled gnats and fleas and spiders, and when they coughed they came crawling out.

There were lice that infested their hair until their eyebrows were swarming, and their eyes closed under the weight of the lice hanging from their lashes. There were lice in their clothes and in their beds. They shaved their hairs. They threw off their clothes and went naked and shameless, screaming in the streets. But still the bugs attached themselves to their tender skin and bit and itched and crawled and squished until they nearly went mad.

They begged their Pharaoh to do whatever it took, to promise whatever he must, but to convince Musa ﷺ to dispel the vermin. Musa ﷺ, in spite of the fact that Pharaoh had consistently broken every promise he had made, once more asked his Lord to remove the infestation. The bugs disappeared and the poor Egyptian people tried to pick up their dignity and rebuild their lives and go on. But did Pharaoh change? No, certainly not. He remained as obstinate as ever. As soon as the plague had passed, he put his promises out of his mind. Bugs had come and gone before; they are part of the natural cycle of the world.

So the next time Allah sent the frogs. First there were just a few of them hopping from the river, a few in the garden, a few on the road. But these few increased, until there were many, and then there were so many, and then there were too many. Everywhere they turned there were heaps and piles of slimy, croaking frogs. The ground was covered. There was no place to walk. The beds, the chairs, the plates, the cups, were all full of frogs. A man would sit down to rest and in a few minutes he would be up to his chin in frogs. If he opened his mouth to speak or eat, the frogs would jump in. If he lay down he would be blanketed in so many frogs that he could not move or hardly breathe. If his wife tried to make bread there would be dozens of small frogs kneaded into the dough.

The din of the croaking in itself was horrible. People ran with their fingers in their ears so as not to hear the croak, croak, ribbet, ribbet, of the frogs and toads. Only the houses of the Banu Israil were free of frogs. Once more Pharaoh asked, and once more Musa ﷺ prayed. Allah Almighty removed the frogs and once more Pharaoh broke his oath. Frogs had come and gone before.

Now Allah offered a new sign, one that would be harder to explain away as a natural occurrence. The people of Egypt woke up one morning to find all the water in Egypt had turned blood red. When the water carriers stooped to fill their jugs from the great river, they found thick, red, blood dripping from their cups. They drew back in horror. When the farmers' daughters threw their buckets into the wells they drew up buckets of dark, gooey clots. When the master of the house poured himself a cup from the water-skin hanging in the shade of his garden, crimson blood poured from its neck as if it had been newly slaughtered.

The Children of Israil did not experience the same thing. In their huts by the river they drew water and drank and noticed nothing amiss. Their neighbors came to them running, begging for them to give them clean water to drink and to wash off the blood. But when the Banu Israil generously poured water for their masters and their neighbors, as soon as it touched their hands or their lips it became gory.

This was not a natural event. Nothing like this had ever been seen before in all the long history of Egypt. There were no steles carved with accounts of such an event, no murals painted with scenes such as they now witnessed. How were they going to explain this? It must, it could only be Musa ﷺ whose curses were causing this to happen. He was bad luck and an evil sorcerer. If they could get rid of him, they would rid themselves of all the evils. For the sixth time they went to Musa ﷺ and begged him to ask for the river to be restored to its natural consistency.

These six, plus the staff that turned into a dragon and the shining hand, comprise eight of the nine signs that are mentioned explicitly in The Quran. The Tawrah enumerates ten signs or plagues. There are also some differences in the numbering of the signs, for instance the drought and the flood might be considered as one, famine. Two additional signs are described below that some Muslim chroniclers include and some do not. Allah knows best. The point is that for many years the Egyptian people were made to suffer under these heaven-sent plagues, until they were exhausted.

As soon as the water became water again the Egyptians went back to their old ways. So Allah ordered the animals of the desert to invade the habitations of people. The wolf, the lion, the jackal, the crocodile, crawled, padded, leaped, and slithered into the secured homes of the people. They bit their children and ate their livestock. They frightened them on their way to the fields and the temples and on their way to seek food and water. After seven days Allah sent the wild animals back to their desert homes. Then the domestic animals began to sicken and die: First one, then the whole herd. The sheep, the goats, the cows, the bulls, even the dogs and cats, lay dying in the sun. No one could do anything to help them and the smell of death hung like a cloud over the land. After seven days the dying ceased but still the Egyptians refused to heed.

In another sign sometimes mentioned, Allah hid the sun, the giver of warmth, of light, of life. Darkness enveloped Egypt. It was so dark they couldn't see their hands in front of their faces. They couldn't find the door to go outside. They couldn't even tell the outside from the inside. And this darkness was no ordinary darkness. If they lit a lamp the flame was immediately sucked into the darkness. It absorbed all light into itself, and all sound. It hung heavy in the air until the people found it difficult to draw breath. There was no sound, no sight, just heavy darkness. Terror spread through the hearts of all the people. There was nowhere to escape. For three days and three nights they endured this trial and yet when it was lifted, they returned to their old ways without repentance or remorse.

"And verily We sent Musa with Our revelations to Pharaoh and his chiefs, and he said: I am a Messenger of the Lord of the Worlds. But when he brought them Our signs, behold, they laughed at them." (43:46-47)

Eight signs had been delivered. Eight signs had been ignored. There was still one sign remaining to be shown.

27.

A Community Of Believers

Although Pharaoh remained obstinate and unbelieving during and after these many trials, a number of the ordinary people saw the signs and heeded the warnings. These people came in secret, at night or in the early morning, to visit the prophets. Allah instructed Musa ﷺ to designate special houses in which people could gather and pray together and sit in association, learning wisdom from their prophets. They were not ordered to build temples or mosques, but to use ordinary houses that did not attract the attention of the Pharaoh or his men. In just this way the Prophet Muhammad ﷺ used the house of Arqam ﷺ as a meeting place for the first believers in the early days in Mecca.

"And We inspired Musa and his brother: Appoint houses for your people in Egypt and make your houses places of worship, and establish prayer. And give good news to the believers." (10:87)

The new believers were mostly from among the youth of the Banu Israil, who had forgotten their own traditions and grown up following Egyptian customs and beliefs. The goal of their fathers had been to disappear and merge with the general Egyptian population. They had rejected the practices that made them different, even if it made them right. Most of the tribes of Israil had abandoned the way of Yusuf ﷺ and they followed the way of unbelief. Only the tribe of Lavi had kept to the religion and their elders continued to protect as much as they could of

"and make your houses places of worship, and establish prayer." (10:87)

the traditions and wisdom handed down from the prophets of the past. Now the children and grandchildren of all the tribes felt drawn to seek out the abandoned knowledge of their ancestors and renew their covenant with the God of Ibrahim ﷺ, Ya'qub ﷺ, and Yusuf ﷺ.

There were many of the new communtiy, however, who were people of Egyptian heritage, whose hearts were clean and open to Allah. These men and women heard, in the words of the prophets, an undeniable truth and they were attracted to keep company with the believers. They came in twos and threes to sit at the feet of Musa ﷺ and Harun ﷺ and absorb whatever teaching they could. They pledged themselves to serve only one God and to defend His prophets and His people. The new community accepted them into itself.

This growing community did not go unnoticed. Pharaoh and Haman heard rumors of the growing numbers of believers. To discourage such behavior, the government issued orders for all employers and overseers to crack down on the Children of Israil. They forced the slaves to work under even more unbearable conditions, and beat them unmercifully if they faltered. They sought out the freeborn Egyptian sons and daughters who were converting, and imprisoned them in their houses and tried to make them deny their faith. They acted in much the same manner as the unbelievers of Quraysh were to act many centuries later to the first Muslims in Mecca.

As a consequence, the immediate result of the preaching and ministry of Musa ﷺ and Harun ﷺ was that, instead of bettering the conditions of their people, it made conditions much worse. The Banu Israil started to complain.

"They said: We suffered hurt before you came to us, and since you have come to us." (7:129)

"You were supposed to make things easier, to be our saviors and our rescuers," they said. "But you have only made things worse. We wish you would go away and leave us. We will do what the Egyptians want us to do. We will become what they want us to become. No harm will be done and maybe we will be happy." After all those years of oppression they had developed a slave mentality; they no longer stood up for what they knew was right, but instead sought the easiest path out of their difficulties.

Although a son of Israel by birth, Musa ﷺ had been educated as an Egyptian prince and raised in the palace surrounded by luxury and privilege. He had not tasted the servitude of his people or the injustice or the torment. He had certainly gotten a taste of difficulty since he had left the palace but the people knew nothing of this and it meant nothing to them. If he was truly the one sent by God to lead them to freedom then he was also the one because of whom the Pharaoh had killed all those boy children. And if he was not their redeemer, then his speech and actions were now resulting in more death, loss and hardship. Either way, they could bear no more. Few of the mature generation of Banu Israil were willing to take a chance and put their support behind him.

"But none trusted Musa, except some offspring of his people, in fear of Pharaoh and his supporters that they would persecute them." (10:83)

The strong and the wealthy, who might have been able to stand up to their families and the authorities, were not attracted to this new religion. Either they were selfishly content with the status quo or, in their arrogance, they thought that they had earned whatever good they possessed. They felt no need for other than what they already had. The ones who did believe, tried to save themselves by hiding behind their wealth and social standing, but they were unable to hide for long. Asiya ﵟ, even though she was the Queen, when she had dared to stand up to her husband, had been treated in the same manner as the magicians and slaves. Her wealth and status had availed her nothing and in fact probably led to even more severe punishment.

The only ones who dared to publicly support the

prophets were either the very young, whose idealism outweighed their fear, or the very weak, who had nowhere to hide and nothing to lose. The rest of the nation followed their Pharaoh into disbelief and disaster. Pharaoh and his court, whenever they had the chance, taunted Musa ﷺ and Harun ﷺ. Pharaoh said,

> "I am better than this fellow, who is contemptible, and can hardly make (his meaning) plain. Why, then, have bracelets of gold not been set upon him, or angels sent along with him? Thus he (pharaoh) persuaded his people to make light of Musa and they obeyed him." (43:52-55)

They dismissed these men of God because they were not possessed of material power and wealth. They confused the two worlds thinking that the things they admired and desired, golden ornaments and social status, were the things of real value. All the while, God was telling them that a true heart and a grateful soul rank higher with Him than all the treasures on earth. They felt that the new religion was not worthy of their respect or attention because its prophets and most of its followers, were weak, of low social rank, poor, young, or female.

This was also the case when the Prophet Muhammad ﷺ first began preaching. He had very few followers among his family or social equals, only Hamza ﷺ and AbuBakr ﷺ. The rest of the Muslims were the young, the women, and the slaves. They were easily tortured for their beliefs, imprisoned and even killed. It was said about the Prophet ﷺ as well, even though he was of the noblest lineage but because he was orphaned and poor. Prophecy should have been granted to a man of greater social or political substance. As if they would have listened if the revelation had issued from the mouth of their chief.

> "And now that the Truth has come unto them they say: This is mere magic, and verily, we are disbelievers in it. And they say: If only this Quran had been revealed to some great man of

the two towns (Mecca and Taif)." (43:30-31)

So the people of Egypt mostly consented to follow Pharaoh. They laughed at the believers because they were not of the powerful class. They dismissed the divine message and the miracles with which it had been sent, as magic and therefore a lie. If any disaster happened they blamed the prophets for cursing them or bringing bad luck. If anything good happened they called it a natural event that would have occurred in spite of the presence of the prophets. But Allah Almighty gave them the chance to choose the right way and hoped that His beloved creation would live up to the perfect form in which He had created them.

"Otherwise, if disaster should afflict them because of that which their own hands have sent before them, they might say: O our Lord, why did You not send any messengers to us, that we might have followed Your revelation and been among the believers? But when there came to them the Truth (The Quran) from Our Presence, they said: Why is he not given the like of what was given to Musa? Did they not disbelieve in that which was given to Musa of old? They say: Two magics that support each other; and they say: Verily in both we are disbelievers." (28:47-48)

משה

27/48

28.

Buried Treasure

Among the Banu Israil there were those who profited personally from the enslavement of their own people. They were wealthy men, occupying positions of power, who took pride in having overcome their origins and having risen above their people. One such man was Qarun, or Korah as he was known to the Hebrews. He was a very wealthy man and a close relative, a first cousin on their father's side, of Musa ﷺ and Harun ﷺ.

In the Hadith the companions of the Prophet Muhammad ﷺ are recorded as having said that not forty, or even sixty, gray mules with white blazes on their foreheads could have carried the saddlebags containing just the keys to the treasure rooms of Qarun. In other accounts seventy camels were unable to rise from their knees under the weight of those keys, each of which was made of leather and only the size of a finger. In The Quran it says that the wealth of Qarun was such that a troop of powerful men would have been burdened by having to transport the keys to his treasure. Because of this great wealth, and despite his origins, he had a high social position and political power. He had no interest in reviving the old traditions, or the old beliefs that he thought had contributed to the subjugation of his people. He dressed as an Egyptian, ate and lived as an Egyptian. There was no way to tell that he was other than an Egyptian. And when it came to decisions about the welfare of his people, he also thought like an Egyptian.

It might have been that he tried to alleviate some of the suffering of his people by convincing the authorities to soften

"So We caused the earth to swallow him." (28:81)

their treatment of the Banu Israil. Maybe he even gave, out of his vast treasures, some charity and aid to the families who were in such need. But his preferred solution to the problem was for the Banu Israil to give up their ways and follow the Egyptian ways, to merge with the larger population as he had. So when Musa ﷺ came with orders to revive the old religion, to refresh their memory of the old ways, he came into direct confrontation with Qarun. He was advising the very things that Qarun had struggled so hard to forget and to discard.

Qarun probably thought of himself as the savior of his people with no need for Musa ﷺ. And the people themselves thought of him as their chief and the one they went to for counsel and for help. So when Musa ﷺ came with a contradictory message he was in effect, placing himself in competition with Qarun for honor and power.

Allah mentions Qarun together with Haman and Pharaoh, as the three enemies of God. For different reasons they all were on the same side. Where Musa ﷺ should have had an ally he had instead an enemy, not only in the palace but also in the houses of his people. Qarun's influence was great and there were many indebted to him. The Banu Israil did not flock to support Musa ﷺ and Harun ﷺ. The majority of the Banu Israil tried, as best they could, to keep their heads down and avoid being noticed. They admired and envied Qarun. He had wealth and luxury. He had power and privilege. He was free. His path was the one successful path that they could see.

Musa ﷺ always spoke to his people about charity. Charity is a cover and a protection for the believers. Allah asked for the believers to pay a tax on their property that could be used by the state for those in need. At the time of Musa ﷺ the believers were asked to pay one quarter of the value of their wealth into a treasury. The name for this tax is 'zakat' which is derived from the word meaning to cleanse or purify. Its purpose is both to support those in need and to clean the wealth of those with excess. In reality it is a charity for everyone.

When Qarun heard this he was incensed. He had

amassed a fortune in every kind of treasure but he could not find it in his heart to give anything away for nothing. He opened one box and ran his fingers through the coins – no, he could not part with these. He opened another box and tried on the various rings and jewels. No, these he could not do without. He opened another box and dangled the necklaces studded with gems. No, he might have need of these sometime in the future. No, he had nothing to give. He needed all that he had. He hated Musa ﷺ for torturing him with this order to give; and he hated that, as a consequence, he looked cheap and ungenerous to the people. But he hated even more to lose anything of the things he had collected. Even though, at Musa's ﷺ request, Allah Almighty reduced the amount required from Qarun from one fourth to one fortieth, then to one hundredth, finally to one thousandth. Still Qarun could not bear to part with one diadem, or one earring, or one gold tooth.

Qarun decided that the time had come to destroy his enemy, Musa ﷺ, once and for all. It was a feast day for one of the many gods of the Egyptians. People, Egyptians as well as Banu Israil, collected offerings and went to the temples to praise and adorn the animal-headed gods. Musa ﷺ and Harun ﷺ also went to the temple to try to talk sense into the people. How could they worship a statue made by their own hands and refuse the worship of the One who had made them. These statues could neither help them nor hurt them. A crowd of supporters and detractors had gathered to listen to or to mock the wisdom they relayed.

Qarun, dressed in robes of purple and gold, arrived in his golden chariot, which was drawn by horses whose reins and bridles were of gold. It jingled with golden ornaments and bright purple tassels. Seventy slave girls, dressed to match him in purple and gold, ran beside his chariot. His only purpose was ostentation. He thought that his wealth and power were an indication of God's approval, rather than the test that they truly were. The people made way for him and admired him, and wished in their hearts that they could be like him. He was carried by his slaves from his carriage to the top of the temple steps, where he stood next to the prophets, Musa ﷺ and Harun ﷺ.

"Then he went forth before his people in his pomp. Those who were desirous of the life of the world said: Ah, would that unto us had been given the like of what has been given to Qarun! Lo he is lord of rare good fortune." (28:79)

He began to address Musa ﷺ as if he needed an urgent answer to a question. "O Prophet of God," he said. "What is the punishment for adultery?" Musa ﷺ replied as his Lord instructed him. "The guilty ones are to be pelted with stones until they are dead." Then Qarun made a sign with his hand and a pregnant woman laboriously mounted the steps to stand beside them.

The people gasped and Qarun could hardly contain his joy. This was his plan. He had paid the woman well to tell the people that it was Musa ﷺ who was the father of her unborn child. But as the woman tried to speak her tongue twisted in her mouth and she was unable to form the words of the lie she had agreed to tell. So Qarun spoke the words for her.

Musa ﷺ was a strong man, maybe no prophet before or after was as strong as he. His anger was so powerful that even his more powerful will was unable to conceal it. His face darkened like a storm over an already raging sea, and his whole body shook with fury. He prayed to his Lord to defend His servant with the truth.

Some say that Allah transported the shepherd, who was the true father of the child, to the temple steps and he testified to his act of adultery. Some say that the unborn child was given a voice that could be heard throughout the assembly and he identified his true father, praised the Lord, and declared the innocence of the Prophet Musa ﷺ.

Allah then put the whole earth under the command of Musa ﷺ. Musa ﷺ ordered Qarun to admit to his lie. But Qarun was too stubborn. So Musa ﷺ ordered the earth to swallow

Qarun and his men. Slowly what was once firm ground began to suck at their feet and the men sank into the earth up to their ankles. Qarun was terrified and offered to pay whatever charity tax Musa ﷺ asked for. But Musa ﷺ was still angry. He ordered the earth to swallow them up to their knees. Qarun offered more money. Musa ﷺ ordered them to be swallowed to the waist, then to the shoulders, then to the chin, then to the mouth. Still, with just their mouths above ground, their eyes imploring, they begged for mercy. Then they were gone, buried alive in the belly of the earth. They say that still today, in each minute they are sinking deeper, the earth is still dragging them inch-by-inch, ever closer to its fiery core.

"So We caused the earth to swallow him and his dwelling place. Then he had no host to help him against Allah, nor was he of those who can save themselves." (28:81)

Afterwards Allah reprimanded His Prophet ﷺ. Seven times Qarun had pleaded with Musa ﷺ for mercy, and seven times Musa ﷺ had turned a deaf ear. If Qarun had only turned to Allah, the All Merciful, and asked even just once, Divine Mercy would surely have been showered upon him. But because he was not of those who can save themselves by asking humbly for forgiveness from his Creator, Qarun suffered a fate worse than death.

Even after this terrible sign the people still found doubt easier than belief and they began to grumble that Musa ﷺ had only destroyed Qarun because he wanted his money. So Musa ﷺ went to the palace of Qarun, where all of his treasure chests were stored. The people watched as the whole building and all its golden contents followed their master into the depths of the earth. Musa ﷺ did this in order to show the people the true value of material wealth in the eyes of God and His prophets. In the same way the Prophet Muhammad ﷺ refused the kingship and wealth offered him by the Meccans if he would only agree to stop preaching a new religion. And later, when sent many camel loads of treasure, he turned it all into sand so that it would not become a temptation for the Muslims.

29.

Towering Arrogance

Pharaoh and Haman had lost a most valuable ally in Qarun. Pharaoh was getting desperate, and foolishness is bound to follow in the footsteps of desperation. He ordered Haman to gather the slaves and make them work day and night to form bricks of mud. With these bricks Pharaoh ordered them to build a tower so high that he could mount into the Heavens and take a peak to see if the God of Musa ﷺ was really there. This demented plan was the ultimate in materialist foolishness.

"And Pharaoh said: O Haman! Build for me a tower that I may reach the roads, the roads of the Heavens, and may look upon the God of Musa, though, honestly I think he is a liar." (40:36-37)

It took many months but finally the tower was built. Pharaoh was carried on the backs of his slaves to the terrace on the very top. From there he shot an arrow into the sky. He said that it fell back to earth tipped in blood. This, Pharaoh claimed, was the blood of the God of Musa ﷺ. He announced that he had killed the God of Israil and, as a result, he remained the only god standing. But this arrogant ploy did nothing to change the situation.

The members of the government and the family of the Pharaoh began to be concerned by the behavior of their king. A council was called to discuss what was to be done. Haman suggested to Pharaoh that the time had come to eliminate the

"I am your lord most high." (79:24)

root of the problem. The time had come to kill Musa ﷺ himself. Pharaoh whole-heartedly agreed. They began to discuss the best way to carry out this murderous plot.

But one of the men among the close family of Pharaoh was secretly a believer in the message of Musa ﷺ and Harun ﷺ. When he heard his family conspiring to kill the prophets, he could no longer keep his secret or hold his tongue. Beside himself with indignation and righteous anger, he stood up in the council. First he tried to reason with them. He said,

"Would you kill a man because he says 'My Lord is God,' while he brought you clear proofs from your Lord? And if he should be lying, then his lie is upon him, while if he should be truthful, there will befall you something of that which he promises you. Indeed, God does not guide one who is a transgressor and a liar." (40:28)

Whatever your problems with this man, he said, he has not broken any law by believing in God. All the Egyptians believe in a god. This is not a legitimate reason to kill someone. If he is right, and he has certainly brought enough signs to make that a possibility, then you would be best served by listening to him and the fact that he is warning you is a commendable thing. If he is wrong then there is nothing to worry about, he hurts no one but himself. Leave him alone and let his God take care of him if he lies. He cannot harm you.

We do not know who this man was, his age, or his name but he must have been someone very close to Pharaoh, well respected and loved, because Pharaoh began to defend and justify his own actions rather than to threaten or shout. He meekly said that he was just doing his best. He had no personal vendetta against Musa ﷺ. He was appointed as the ruler over Egypt, and he was just doing his best to serve his people and guide them correctly.

"Pharaoh said: I do but show you what I think, and I do

but guide you to a wise policy." (40:29)

Then the unknown believer turned to the assembled men, kinsmen and statesmen, throwing open his arms and pleading with them. Maybe he was hoping that Allah would put in his mouth the one word that would open the hearts of his relatives and friends. Maybe he hoped there was something he could say that would avert the punishment he felt sure was looming over his arrogant countrymen. He must have loved them very much to risk everything, including his life, to try to open their eyes. He reminded them of the other prophets who had come before and of their nations who were destroyed because they rejected them.

"O my people pleaded the believer, indeed, I fear for you a fate like that of the factions of old; a plight like that of Noah's people and 'Ad and Thamud and those after them. And God desires no injustice for His servants. And, O my people, indeed I fear for you a Day of Summoning – a day when you will turn to flee, having no protector against God. And whomever God leaves astray, for him there is no guide." (40:30-33)

The believer reminded them of the prophet whom their own grandfathers had witnessed and respected. Remember Yusuf ﷺ, he said. Remember Yusuf ﷺ who brought you this very same message. The believer could not let the matter rest. He had revealed himself, now he must put before his people every sound argument he could think of.

He reminded them that this life is short but the afterlife is eternal. This was, after all, the very foundation of Egyptian belief. What difference if they had money to build an enormous tomb full of treasure and provision for a body that was no longer in need and a soul that required none of those things? If they had prepared no goodness or kindness or justice, if their hearts were like stone, unthankful for all the blessings their Creator had given them, then they had nothing.

The believer spoke with great eloquence and emotion. How is it that Allah and His prophets were calling them to justice and to goodness and they were inviting their people to injustice and to wickedness? How is it that they, who were sensible people, good people in all other ways, were so blind to this simple fact? How is it that they could not see? Never did God destroy a people before they had been warned. Here was their warning, loud and clear, in their own language, spoken by a friend and a relative. It was not a threat of political upheaval or revolution. The speaker was one of their own, on their side. But to no avail, no one listened.

The Prophet Muhammad ﷺ spent ten years in his native land of Mecca trying to talk to his neighbors and kinsmen about the truths and wisdoms being revealed through him. He found very few who would listen and fewer still who would believe. Year after year he endured their insults and mockery, which escalated into physical abuse and harassment. Finally his people decided to kill him. At that point he and the believers were delivered from Mecca into a new land and eventually given victory over their oppressors.

For forty years Musa ﷺ and Harun ﷺ were ordered by Allah Almighty to continue pleading with Pharaoh. Allah loves His creation and does not destroy it easily. Pharaoh had been chosen and given great favors in this world. He was given extraordinary wealth, power, authority, and worldly eminence. He was given health and strength, intelligence and charisma. He was loved and obeyed by thousands of his people. In return he had governed his people with mercy and justice. He had built beautiful cities and majestic monuments. He had brought peace, law, and order to a great empire covering much of Africa and the Middle East. He had behaved as a responsible deputy of God Almighty for many, many years.

"What concern has Allah for your punishment if you are thankful and believe?" (4:147)

Then Pharaoh's fear got the best of him. He began to fear his mortality. He attempted to protect himself from death, and from destiny. He began to play with fate and to try to eliminate what he saw as the threat of the Banu Israil. But even his tyranny and fear attested to his inner conviction that there was a God Whose power and purpose were independent of his own. He was trying to convince himself, with all his might, that he was a god. In the beginning of his challenge with Musa ﷺ he only said:

"O nobles, I know no god for you other than me." (28:38)

But now he stood up and shouted:

"I am your god most high." (79: 24)

This attested, clearly and unequivocally, to the fact that all the efforts of God and His prophets had only increased Pharaoh in denial and disbelief. He had been given more than a fair chance and it had only encouraged his ignorance and arrogance. The prophets had reached the end of their tolerance. They asked their Lord to stop Pharaoh and their plea was accepted.

"And Musa said: 'Our Lord, You have given Pharaoh and his men splendor and riches in the life of this world, Our Lord, that they may lead men astray from Your way. Our Lord, destroy their riches and harden their hearts so that they believe not till they see a painful doom.' He [Allah] said: 'Your prayer is heard.'" (10:88-89)

At this point Allah told Musa ﷺ and Harun ﷺ to prepare themselves and their people; the time for leaving Egypt was at hand.

30.

Finding Yusuf ﷺ

Musa ﷺ warned that one final sign was yet to be delivered by the Lord. This was his last warning to the people of Pharaoh. He told the believers to prepare to travel. It was clear to most of the Banu Israil at this point, whether they believed or not, that Egypt was no longer a safe place to bring up their children or to live their lives. However unsure they were of where their prophets were leading them, it would be better than the injustice and tyranny of Pharaoh. They had no choice now but to follow their kinsmen wherever the Lord would lead them.

Musa ﷺ instructed the Banu Israil to pack up their belongings, being careful not to attract the attention of their neighbors. They should appear to go about their chores and business as usual. They should make bread for the journey but make it without yeast so that they would not have to set it in the sun to rise or to fire the big wood ovens to bake it. Rather they should make cracker bread on flat stones over the small hearths within the walls of their houses. This way no one would become suspicious and guess that they were planning for a long journey.

He also instructed them, on the orders of Allah Almighty, to go to their Egyptian neighbors and say that they would all be leaving in a few days to attend a festival held in the countryside outside of town. They would like to borrow the customary golden ornaments and jewelry worn on these occasions. The Egyptians had conceived a general fear of the Banu Israil after all of the plagues and ordeals that had affected the free men but not their slaves. They gave them whatever they

The stone coffin of Yusuf ﷺ made its way slowly to the surface.

asked for thinking that they would have no trouble getting it back.

The Banu Israil were ordered to pack this treasure and take it with them for they had no gold or money of their own. This was divine justice. This gold and treasure was recompense for all the years of work they and their ancestors had done without either wages or payment of any kind. Some say that when Yusuf ﷺ was in charge of the finances of Egypt he had collected so much wealth in gold, silver and precious gems that it still filled the treasure houses of Egypt. The wealth the Banu Israil took rightfully belonged to his descendants and was a gift of kindness from their Generous Lord.

When this was accomplished, the prophets told them that, in the night, Allah would send the Angel of Death to take the firstborn of every living thing. The only protection for the believers was to sacrifice an animal and smear its blood over the door of their houses. The Angel of Death would see the blood, recognize the house of a believer, and pass over it.

There was just one more thing that had to be done. The Prophet Yusuf ﷺ, before he died, had made his children promise that when the expected prophet came to lead them out of Egypt they would take his remains with them. Now it was an obligation on Musa ﷺ, as a descendant of Yusuf ﷺ, to fulfill this promise.

The problem was that no one remembered where

Yusuf ﷺ had been buried. He was so beloved that every group wanted the benefits of being near his blessed body. Everyone wanted him buried near their tomb, near their ancestors. The children of Yusuf ﷺ were so afraid that people would fight over him or disturb his resting place that they buried his coffin at night somewhere under the flowing water of the Nile. This way everyone would receive the benefit of being near him and no one could claim him exclusively.

But now no one remembered where he had been buried. Musa ﷺ sent men to every house of the Banu Israil to ask if anyone knew anything or remembered having heard their grandfathers say anything, about the burial of Yusuf ﷺ. But the men came back one after the other, empty handed, without a clue, and it began to look hopeless.

At last someone said that they had heard that there was a very, very old lady living by herself in a hut on the edge of the desert and she was always trying to tell the children stories of things that had happened long ago. She might remember something. She was not, however, a descendant of Yaqub ﷺ. She was an Egyptian of the family of Asiya ؇, the Queen. Her grandfathers had been followers of Yusuf ﷺ and they had held anything that had to do with him in the highest respect. Every word they heard him speak, every action they saw him make, they remembered and told their children and grandchildren. She had tried to preserve this knowledge, but she had not found anyone in the recent past who would listen to her.

Musa ﷺ went to visit her himself. He found her sitting warming herself in the sun. She was nearly blind and almost deaf and she could hardly stand and certainly not walk. He approached her and greeted her loudly, in God's name. When she finally understood, her little wrinkled face lit up. Yes she did know the place where the Prophet Yusuf ﷺ was laid to rest. She had heard her grandfather tell the story many times and her grandmother had pointed out the place whenever they took the ferry across the river to market. If Musa ﷺ would carry her on his back she would try to lead him to the spot.

Musa ﷺ lifted the little old lady on his strong back and carried her where she directed him. She asked that if she found the burial place would he agree to take her with him out of Egypt? Musa ﷺ agreed. Then she asked in addition, after she had died and been resurrected again with a spiritual body of light, would he take her to be one of his wives in the gardens of Paradise? Musa ﷺ smiled and agreed to this request as well.

The old lady directed him to a place on the shore of the Nile where the river curves and there were small sailboats for hire. They boarded one and told the boatman to sail towards the middle of the great river. After what seemed to her to be the right length of time, the old lady said that this was the place where the coffin of Yusuf ﷺ had been lowered into the river. Musa ﷺ raised his hands and prayed for help. Then he touched the river with his staff. A circle of water began to bubble and boil. Faintly they could see through the blue water a stone coffin making its way slowly toward the surface. When it broke through the surface of the water Musa ﷺ grabbed it with the hook on the back of his staff and pulled it close to the boat where it miraculously floated. Keeping a firm grip on it in this way, they sailed with it back to the bank and hid the coffin carefully in the reeds by the shore where the great river makes a bend close to the road.

There is a lesson in this for all of us. The stories of the grandfathers, the tales of the grandmothers should be listened to with attention and respect. The wisdom of the elderly is more precious than gold. Concealed within the words of the elderly are wisdom, humor, and hope. Like seeds, they remain buried in the fertile ground of the young mind until the appropriate time comes for them to appear and flourish. No one knows what knowledge will be useful to him in the future. The words of the wise are precious seeds from which the future is grown.

31.

The Ninth Sign

The next day the Banu Israil finished all their preparations. They packed their cracker bread in big sacks. They borrowed the golden jewelry of their neighbors and overseers. The men slaughtered whatever animal they could afford and with their hands smeared the blood over the doorways of their houses. Then they sat quietly inside their homes, old and young, infant and grandma, and they anxiously waited.

As night fell they could hear a frightful noise; it was the wild wind arising from the beating wings of the Angel of Death as he went from door to door looking for the firstborn. The Angel took the firstborn human and animal of every household not marked by the blood of sacrifice. The Children of Israil could hear the shrieks and cries as mothers saw their children stricken dead. They could hear the bellowing and screeching of the animals as their calves and kids, chicks and lambs fell to the ground never to move again. This was the ninth and last warning sign. There was still time to change course and obey the Lord. Allah was taking His just revenge for the killing of His chosen people, the ones who, in the Tawrah, he calls His 'firstborn'. The Children of Israil sat on their bags and bundles, huddled together in the dark, their heads bowed, and their hands covering their ears.

Finally the wind died down and an eerie quiet took over, as the mourners, who were too exhausted to cry any longer, began the long process of preparing their dead for the afterlife. This is when the prophets sent runners to signal the believers

"There is no might or strength except in Allah, the High, the Powerful."

to move. In the dead of night the Children of Israil crept from their houses. They left the lamps burning in their windows as if they were still inside. They placed their hands softly over the mouths of their children to muffle their crying. They tried to keep their animals from bleating and the wheels of their wagons were greased to avoid creaking. They met up with their leaders, Musa ﷺ and Harun ﷺ, at the bend in the river where the coffin of Yusuf ﷺ had been hidden earlier in the day.

It was the ninth of the month of Muharram say some scholars. All of the descendants of Yusuf ﷺ, of Ya'qub ﷺ, all twelve tribes of Israil assembled in the presence of their prophets, in the sight of God Almighty, to be led out of Egypt.

Musa ﷺ and Harun ﷺ organized the men of this multitude into battalions and legions. Each of the twelve tribes was placed under the command of their chiefs to protect the women, children, and elderly. In front of the tribes, the coffin of Yusuf ﷺ was placed on a wagon, covered with fine cloths, and carried with honor. The old lady who had remembered his burial place rode beside him, on pillows set inside the bed of the wagon.

Allah took all the believers out of Egypt that night. There were children, who like Musa ﷺ, had been adopted and raised by unbelieving parents. Somehow, by a miracle of God, they were returned to their rightful families and joined the caravan. The believer from the family of Pharaoh safely made his way, with his family, to join the group. The carpenter who, so long ago, had built the box in which Ummi Musa had given up her baby to the rushing currents of the Nile, joined them with his family. Many, many young Egyptians who had been absorbing the truths on the tongues of Allah's prophets and witnessing the many miracles and obvious signs, had also smeared blood on their doorways and gone out with the Banu Israil.

"And verily We revealed to Musa: Travel by night with My servants, then strike for them a dry path in the sea, not fearing to be overtaken, nor being afraid." (20:77)

The Egyptians built all their sacred places, their temples and graveyards, on the west bank of the Nile under the setting sun. Their residences, markets and farms were all on the east bank to greet the rising sun. Leaving the river Nile behind them the believers set out east for the great sea. All of them, Egyptian and Jew, left everything except the few necessities they could carry. They left the houses where they had been born, the fields they and their ancestors had worked. They left the beautiful cities they had helped to build and the temples and public places they had carved and painted with their hands. They left the graves of their ancestors and they left their neighbors; they left the life that, although hard and unjust, was familiar and all they knew. They left everything to follow their prophets into the unknown. Musa ﷺ and Harun ﷺ prayed to their Lord, asking for help.

The Egyptians saw the sun rise that morning, blood red. They were busy preparing their dead for burial and preparing the thousands of graves. From the hut of the poorest serving girl to the palaces of the Pharaoh, there was not one house that was untouched by loss, except the houses of the believers. In this way Allah Almighty kept the enemy busy and preoccupied. They did not notice that some houses were empty and some neighbors missing. They went about the rituals of the dead until the sun was high in the sky. Only then did they begin to notice that all the slaves were missing. They searched and called for them but found only silence.

The scouts of the Pharaoh came galloping at high speed to tell him that they had seen tracks on the road of many men and wagons heading east out of Egypt. The spies soon came running with reports that the prophets were gone and with them all the gold of Egypt. Pharaoh's fury knew no bounds. He commanded his entire army to assemble in front of the palace. He mounted his soldiers on one million, seven hundred thousand horses, all of them pure black stallions. After many hours they were armed and ready. They set out in pursuit of the Banu Israil. They galloped across the sands covering quickly the ground that the tribes, with their children and their elderly, their animals and their laden wagons, had covered so slowly earlier that day.

Before long Musa could see the cloud of dust behind them on the road. Soon they could all see, over their shoulders, the army of Pharaoh quickly approaching. The Children of Israel looked ahead of them and saw the great wide sea. They looked behind them and they saw the sharpened spears of their enemy.

"When the two groups saw each other, Musa's companions said: Surely we are indeed caught." (26:61)

Musa replied, "No, in truth! For My Lord is with me. He will guide me." (26:62)

The Prophet Muhammad once asked his companions if they wanted to know the prayer that Sayyidina Musa prayed before he led his people into the sea. They replied that they did. He told them it was, "Allah, to You alone is all praise; and to You we turn in suffering; You are the One we ask for help; and in You alone do we put our trust. There is no might or strength except in Allah, the High, the Powerful." This remains until today the familiar prayer of the Muslim in need.

The Lord had directed Musa's speech and his actions for over forty years, had delivered miracles to support him, had put the earth at his command, and now had promised him safety and victory. Musa was concerned at the predicament before him but not daunted and certainly not hopeless or helpless. He climbed up on a promontory above the sea and looked out over the scene.

An Opening In The Sea

Musa ﷺ saw on his right the great sea. It is said that Allah Almighty the night before had sent an angel to address the waters of the sea. "O Sea, Prepare yourself," the angel said, "tomorrow your Lord is putting you under the command of His most obedient servant. You will hear his orders and obey them, exactly as he commands you."

The sea had never received a divine command of this nature and it was anxious and afraid. Its water began to roll and heave until it generated huge waves like mountains, with froth and foam spitting from their peaks. These waves slammed into the shore making a noise like thunder, sending spray and foam in every direction. A wild wind had been called out of the east and it blew the already raging water to even greater heights. All night the sea had been rolling and heaving, its waters crashing into each other in nervousness.

Off in the distance to his left, Musa ﷺ could see the army of Pharaoh, looking like a tornado of dust and sand. The black stallions, decorated in gold and jewels, pulled chariots of gold, each carrying a driver and an archer. Their wheels whipped the sand and pebbles into a storm of dust. The swordsmen rode black stallions, their manes and tails plated with gold, their golden hooves sparking the ground. The infantry ran behind, weapons in hand, massive warriors who knew no fear. The sun glinted off all the gold and freshly sharpened weapons, adding an eerie glow to the storm of dust. These were the fighting forces of Pharaoh and they had conquered all the worlds to the west

"O Abu Khalid, open a way for us."

and to the east and had never been led to defeat.

Between the sea and the Pharaoh, Musa ﷺ saw the believers huddled, inexperienced and unsure. The twelve tribes were grouped under their leaders, each surrounding their defenseless women and children. There were six hundred and twenty thousand men of fighting age but they had never actually fought or been tested. They were farmers and herdsmen, architects and artists. He could see their heads turning right and left, their eyes white with fear, but nowhere did they find an escape; it was either plunge into the roiling waters or face the raging enemy.

Musa ﷺ went down from his vantage point to give courage to his people. As he walked among them he could hardly hear the crying of the babies and the bleating of the animals over the pounding of the surf on the shore and the howling of the wild wind.

Then God inspired Musa ﷺ,

"Strike the sea with your staff," (26:63)

He reached his arm out over the raging waters and struck the great sea with his shepherd's staff. "O Abu Khalid," he said, "O Father of eternity, open a way for us." The sea had been preparing for this moment all night. It was also nervous and afraid. When it heard the Prophet ﷺ address it with such an honorable and ancient title, it calmed down and obeyed. The sea rose high into the sky, one part separated from the other until they stood like two mountains on either side. In the middle ran a path of hard sand, firm like a road. The people could see the fish swimming contentedly behind the walls of water on each side. They would have thought the walls were made of glass but that occasionally a fountain of spray burst from one side or the other.

Musa ﷺ commanded the believers to quickly take the open road through the sea before the armies of Pharaoh could catch up with them. Harun ﷺ took the lead, for the people trusted and loved him. He walked ahead and the people watched, but they were paralyzed with fear. One among them, Yusha son of Nun ﷺ, the bravest of them all, went running, boldly prancing behind Harun ﷺ to show his people that it was safe and could be done.

But the people were filled with terror and once they started moving they wanted to cross as quickly as humanly possible. The ones in the back crowded up on the ones in front. They began to step on each other and the wagons got tangled and people and animals were being crowded and crushed. So Allah commanded the sea to open, not just one, but twelve separate roads, one for each of the tribes of Israil. Then the believers walked calmly and orderly, in single file. They took heart in seeing the other tribes through the walls of water, with the fish swimming in between.

It was only when the last of the believers were stepping out of the sea that Pharaoh arrived at the shore. He was sitting astride his big black stallion and he reined him in sharply to take a good look at this latest miracle. In his arrogance he said to his generals: " Look! The sea recognizes that I am one of the gods and it has opened a way for me to pursue my enemies." And he tried to charge headlong into the sea but his stallion was not as foolish as his master, and he sensed something was not right and would not follow his master's command.

Allah had sent two of His archangels to watch over the happenings that day. Both Jibrail ﷺ and Mikail ﷺ rode heavenly horses that could be sensed by the earthly horses but were invisible to the eyes of men. Jibrail ﷺ, in a black turban with a long tail, was mounted on a beautiful white mare named the 'Horse of Life'. He guided this mare to saunter in front of Pharaoh's stallion, friskily waving her invisible tail in his face. Then they turned quickly and galloped down the path through the sea. The black stallion got a whiff of the perfume of that angelic white mare and he forgot everything else in the whole world. He bounded so suddenly after the white mare that Pharaoh was almost jolted from his saddle. The rest of the army followed their leader and disappeared into the paths between the walls of water. Mikail ﷺ on his horse rode behind them, shouting and urging the last of the Egyptian soldiers into the sea.

When Jibrail ﷺ reached the far side, and there was no one ahead of him; when Mikail ﷺ had reached the near shore, and there was no one behind him; the whole of Pharaoh and his army were contained inside the seabed. Just then they heard a momentous roar and, looking up, Pharaoh saw the walls of water begin to collapse inward. The soldiers felt the spray of the sea and saw the shadow of the waves overhead but there was no time and no place to run for safety.

Jibrail ﷺ waved in Pharaoh's face the paper he had signed so painfully with his hieroglyphic on the night he had hung himself by his beard in supplication to the Lord. And Pharaoh at last recognized what he had refused to recognize before. As his soul took flight Pharaoh cried out,

"There is no god but the God in whom the Children of Israil believe, and I am one of those who surrenders." (10:90). And God answered him, "Now! When up to now you have rebelled and been one of the wrongdoers?" (10:91)

Pharaoh and all his army perished under that sea. They were buried by wave upon wave of water; their horses, their chariots, their weapons, and their vainglorious golden ornaments all washed to the bottom of that mighty sea in one heart stopping moment.

"…and the heaven and the earth wept not for them, nor were they reprieved."(44:29)

Once when Jibrail ﷺ was visiting the Prophet Muhammad ﷺ he told him his account of that terrible moment. He said: "I never hated anyone as much as I hated a Jinni named Iblis, and Pharaoh. You should have seen me as I stuffed mud and pebbles into the mouth of Pharaoh for fear that he would utter some word that would cause Allah Almighty to forgive him". Pharaoh and all of his army, by means of water, entered the fires of Hell.

"He [Pharaoh] and his troops were arrogant in the land without right, and they deemed that they would not be returned to Us. Therefore We seized him and his troops, and flung them into the sea! Then see what was the end of the wrongdoers! And We made them leaders, inviting to the Fire, and on the Day of Resurrection they will not be helped. And We caused a curse to overtake them in this world, and on the Day of Resurrection they will be among the despised." (28:39-42)

Even when testifying to his belief in the Lord Almighty, Pharaoh could not get himself to testify to the prophethood of Musa ﷺ. If he said "There is no god but Allah", even in the very throes of death he could not get his tongue to utter, "and Musa is the Prophet of Allah". He could only say he believed in the God of the Children of Israil. This indicates something less than total submission. In contrast, many years before, when Pharoah's socerers accepted the truth at the cost of their lives, they cried wholeheartedly,

"We believe in the Lord of the Worlds, the Lord of Musa and Harun." (26:47-48)

Most people understand from this that Pharaoh is one of the few who will stay in the punishment of hellfire forever. But there are others who are sure that Pharaoh will be finally forgiven because in his last breath he testified to the Truth, because he did a fair amount of good early in his life, but primarily because Allah says, "My mercy outweighs My wrath." (Hadith Qudsi). Even Pharaoh will eventually taste of the all-encompassing Mercy of his Lord. But Allah knows best.

Allah in His divine and perfect Justice avenged the wrongful murders of the thousands of infant boys of the

Banu Israil. Just as Pharaoh had condemned those innocent babies, without mercy, to be drowned in the river, so now Allah condemned Pharaoh and all his men, without mercy, to the same watery fate.

But even death is not quite the end of the story of Pharaoh. He was drowned in the angry sea, his soul was cursed and despised, but for his body another chapter of the story was also written. God continues to say,

"But this day We save you in your body so that you may be a sign for those after you." (10:92)

The early Islamic historians explained this by the fact that Allah made Pharaoh's decaying corpse wash up on the shore in order to dispel all doubt that he was a god and could not die. But today there is another possible explanation. It also might be that his body was preserved and is now one of the mummies so horribly displayed under a museum's bright lights, naked and ugly, before the eyes of the irreverent and curious. But again, Allah knows best.

33.

The Other Side

Pharaoh and his army perished beneath mountains of water, his vainglory buried under mud and sand. His golden chariots, his fine, black stallions, his million soldiers and all their weapons, all of them gone in an instant. The believers must have stood on the shore, incredulous, as the raging sea covered over their pursuers and the words of the Lord proved true again.

"…And the good word of your Lord was fulfilled for the Children of Israil because of their endurance; and We annihilated [all] that Pharaoh and his people had done…" (7:137)

Now the Banu Israil were free from their oppressors. They had left the gardens of Egypt and the luxuries of civilization. They faced a rocky desert and many of the same challenges their ancestors had faced so long ago. They were in the hands of their Lord and they had as guides not one, but two of His faithful servants. So many miracles had been performed for their benefit. The world had been turned upside down to bring them to the place in which they now were. They had been supported with portents and prophecy. They had been favored above all other peoples at that time.

"And We chose them, with knowledge, above the worlds." (44:32)

"Perhaps your Lord will destroy your enemy and make you viceroys on earth, so that He may see how you behave." (7:129)

In spite of the fact that they had clearly strayed from the straight path of their ancestors; in spite of the fact that they had forgotten much of the teachings, and forsaken most of the practices with which they had been entrusted; in spite of the fact that they did not rush to welcome or support their prophets; in spite of the fact that they had been tested and failed; in spite of all this, the Banu Israil were still chosen and favored by Allah. That is a fact, and Allah needs no reasons for His Love. However, the two verses quoted above give us some clue as to the qualities that Allah valued in them.

Simply, at the end of a very severe and agonizing trial, they were still there, patiently enduring. They were still the pure descendants of a long line of earlier prophets, the chosen of God, to whom Allah had made a promise. He had promised, Ibrahim ﷺ, Ya'qub ﷺ and Yusuf ﷺ to protect and bless their descendants. The Banu Israil had stayed together as a separate community with its own identity. However weak or undeserving they might have been individually, collectively they were still the only ones on earth who held the books and the knowledge of the worship of the One God. In the Tawrah Allah calls them "His firstborn". Endurance and knowledge, these were their inheritance. Now they would be expected to enhance these qualities and live up to the gifts that had been granted them. It was their turn to show that when granted favors they could handle them justly and behave better than Pharaoh. They were told,

"Perhaps your Lord will destroy your enemy and make you viceroys on earth, so that He may see how you behave." (7:129)

They camped for the night by the shore of destruction. It was the tenth of Muharram, and they had not eaten anything since the night before. Up until today, both Jews and Muslims fast on the tenth of Muharram. The Jews fast in memory of the long day their ancestors spent without eating. They fast in thanks for their escape from bondage and for the annihilation of their enemies. The Muslims fast for the same reasons, for it was the day Allah saved the prophets and the believers from their oppressors. But they also fast for the many other miraculous acts of God that took place on that day since the creation of the world.

The earth was created on the tenth of Muharram. Adam ﷺ was forgiven on the tenth of Muharram. The ark of Nuh ﷺ came to rest on Mt. Judi on the tenth of Muharram. Ibrahim ﷺ was saved from the fire of Nimrod on the tenth of Muharram. Yunus ﷺ was released from the belly of the whale on the tenth of Muharram. The Prophet Daud ﷺ was forgiven; Ayoub ﷺ was healed; Ya'qub ﷺ and Yusuf ﷺ were reunited; Isa ﷺ ascended into the heavens; and the world will come to an end on the tenth of Muharram.

It had been ten hours since the Banu Israil had first set foot in the sea, ten hours and their whole world had changed. They were too exhausted to set up camp, too afraid to light campfires and cook food. They broke fast on the cracker bread they had prepared for their journey. The Jews of today still eat unleavened bread in memory of this night. They eat bitter herbs and vegetables to remember the bitterness of the slavery from which they had been released. They eat a brown paste to symbolize the mud from which, for generations, they had formed bricks to bake in the sun to build Egyptian homes. They dip it all in salt water to commemorate the salty tears shed over the killing and torture of their people.

The first phase of Musa's ﷺ mission was over. He had given Pharaoh a fair chance and he had brought the Banu Israil out of slavery. Now his sole desire was to be with his Lord. He spent only as much time as he really needed to get his people arranged and settled and then told them he was leaving. He instructed Harun ﷺ to follow with the tribes after they had rested. The Banu Israil, however, were not content with this arrangement. They were feeling uneasy and insecure in their new circumstances, like caged animals when first released. They wanted their prophet near by. But Musa ﷺ was firm. There was no one and no thing that could stand between him and Allah. He reassured the Banu Israil that he would be gone only thirty days. He promised them he would return. It is possible he left too hastily for later his Lord questioned him about it:

"And what made you hasten from your people, O Musa? He [Musa] said: They are here on my track, and I hastened on to You, my Lord, so that You might be pleased." (20:83-84)

Musa ﷺ told his brother to watch the tribes carefully and not let the unbelievers among them lead the believers astray. There was a village near where they were encamped. The people of this village had a statue of a cow that they worshipped. Some members of the Banu Israil not only admired this statue but actually had the temerity to approach Musa ﷺ and ask if he wouldn't please make an idol like it for them. The effects of so many hundreds of years of subjugation to the Egyptians and of worshiping statues and animal-headed gods did not disappear overnight. As can be imagined Musa ﷺ rebuked them severely. He asked incredulously,

"Shall I seek for you a god other than God, when He has favored you above all creatures? (7:140)

What was he to do with these people? They had hardly been saved from slavery and death for a week and they were already forgetting the One who had saved them. For all these many years Musa ﷺ had been directed on how to talk to and deal with Pharaoh. Now Pharaoh was gone. His task, his mission, had dramatically changed. He needed to know the guidelines for leading his people onward and for establishing an independent community. He took his cloak and his staff and he prepared to head into the wastelands of southern Sinai. He was anxious to get to the familiar spot for a meeting with His Lord.

The Banu Israil stayed by the sea for, it is said, twelve

nights, resting, and feasting. As they felt stronger and safer they began to consider their future and to ask questions. Was Pharaoh, their enemy for so long, really dead? They had lived their whole lives and known no other king. They thought that maybe he really was a god, and immortal. What was to become of them now that they were without homes or livelihoods? Should they establish their own nation in imitation of the Egyptian nation, which was the only model they knew?

To answer the first question, Allah caused the bodies of Pharaoh and his soldiers to rise to the surface in spite of their heavy armor and weapons. The still raging sea spat the bodies upon the shore for all to see their death and decay.

To answer the second question, Allah promised them a land of their own where they would be sovereign. But they would have to take it by force from the tyrants who already occupied it. They were promised their own land but they could not claim it without effort and sacrifice.

To answer the third question, Allah promised them a Book that would contain all they needed to know to discriminate between good and evil and to live in peace and righteousness. However, they must make a solemn promise that once they received this Book, they would abide by its laws.

משה

33/48

34.

Forbidden Gold

Musa ﷺ did not have to accomplish the journey to Mount Tur on foot. Allah Almighty sent His messenger, the angel Jibrail ﷺ, riding the Horse of Life to carry Sayyidina Musa ﷺ to His Divine Presence. Both the horse and his rider were invisible to the Banu Israil, but before he disappeared, Musa ﷺ promised that he would return in thirty days. The majority of the Banu Israil, on account of the fragility of their faith, began to literally count the days until their prophet's return.

Musa ﷺ was fasting and so maybe they also tried to fast. A fasting person sleeps during the afternoon on the day he is fasting. He is wakeful at night long after breaking his fast, and then he sleeps a second time. Maybe because of this, the Children of Israil got confused in their counting. They counted every waking up from sleep as the beginning of a new day. So every day was counted as one and every night was also counted as one. When only fifteen days had actually passed, they had counted thirty and Musa ﷺ, their prophet, the one on whom they depended, was still nowhere in sight.

The days passed slowly and their fears and doubts grew quickly. They began to imagine that Musa ﷺ had deserted them, or that His Lord had taken him to Himself, or because of their countless sins had punished him. Whatever bad thing could be imagined, they imagined. They began to look about them to find something to distract them and to make them feel secure, something to replace their prophet. Their fearfulness was once again leading them into trouble.

Out of the fire emerged a golden calf, perfect and pleasing.

At the time of Musa's ﷺ birth, Pharaoh was putting to death in alternate years all the boy babies born to the daughters of Israil. Some of the mothers who found their newborns to be boys, took them up into the dry hills that border the cultivated areas around the Nile. They found small caves high up in the face of the rock cliff, too far for any crying to reach the ears of people and safe from predatory animals. They tightly swaddled their babies and, closing the opening of the caves with rocks, they left them.

Every morning early, and every evening late, these mothers climbed the cliff to nurse their baby sons. Some days it was not possible to leave the city undetected. Some nights there were Egyptian guards preventing the people from moving about freely. But the babies grew and flourished despite these interruptions in their feeding. The mothers did not know but Allah was sending His messenger, the Archangel Jibrail ﷺ, to these babies every day. They sucked milk and honey from the wingtips of Allah's angelic servant.

After the year of killing ended and the year of reprieve began, the mothers brought their babies down from the cave and introduced them quietly among their other children. Nobody noticed, or at least nobody asked questions or made trouble. The boys continued to grow among the other children within their families but in some ways they remained very special. They had been suckled on heavenly food and some were able to hold on to their awareness of the spiritual world longer than other people.

One of these boys, now a grown man called as-Samiri, saw the Prophet Musa ﷺ mount the Horse of Life behind the Archangel ﷺ. As-Samiri was not sure what it was that he saw, but he knew it was a blessed being from the spiritual world. He ran quickly to the spot and scooped up some of the sand on which the Horse of Life had stepped. He wrapped it in the tail of his turban and tied it securely.

There are two kinds of emotion that in English are both called by the same name, fear. One kind of fear is a weakness that drives the individual to search for support wherever he can find it. The other kind of fear is a strength: It is the fear of doing wrong or of hurting others. Those among the Banu Israil who were open to rebellion, knew the mild temper of Harun ﷺ and did not fear to displease him. Lacking this good kind of fear, some of them began to question the orders they had been given. They saw the bodies of the Egyptians washing up on the shore laden with golden chains and armor, swords with golden handles, arrows with golden tips. What could be the harm in taking this treasure and saving it for the future?

Harun ﷺ reminded them that the spoils of war were not legal for them. All of it belonged to the state, not to the individual warriors. This way there could be no personal gain involved in the acts of war. In addition, if the enemy was the enemy of God and stricken with His wrath then nothing they left behind them, not their gold, not their houses, not their animals, were permissible for the believers. Because nothing good could come of it, all of it must be destroyed along with the transgressing people. But most of the Banu Israil did not listen. They took it anyway until each of them had amassed a small fortune.

Harun ﷺ, and the firm believers who supported him, were horrified at the actions of their brothers. What they were doing was forbidden. Wasn't it enough that Allah had bequeathed to them the riches of their landlords and taskmasters? Wasn't all the wealth and jewels that they had carried out of Egypt enough for them? They protested, they condemned, and finally they threatened. The rebellious ones submitted only then out of fear. Harun ﷺ ordered them to collect all the illegal wealth that had been stripped off the bloated bodies of the enemies of God, and bury it in the sand. Then he ordered them to build a big bonfire over the spot and burn the gold to ashes.

The people were not very strong in their rebellion nor were they very sure in their unbelief. They were just weak, impatient, and without strong leadership. In addition they were not sure what to do with all the treasure. They had no places to store it and it was not feasible to move freely with golden chariots and heavy gold ornaments. So eventually they accepted Harun's ﷺ authority and the imposing support of his followers. They repented to the Lord, gathered the plunder in a pile and set it on fire. But of course gold does not burn; it only melts and as-Samiri was standing by watching and thinking.

All of a sudden as-Samiri untied his turban and threw the handful of sand into the raging fire. He was not sure what exactly would happen but he knew that there was great power in it. And he wished for a beautiful god of gold to appear out of the fire; a god like the ones he had seen. A god truer than the Egyptian gods, but in an image he could understand and appreciate.

However, some say that as-Samiri was a skilled metal smith. He could make anything out of copper, silver or gold. After the bonfire burned itself out he took the molten gold from the sand and crafted by hand the image of a beautiful calf. Inside it he put the sand he had retrieved from under the hoof of the angelic horse.

"I perceived what they perceived not, so I seized a handful from the footsteps of the messenger, and then threw it in. Thus my ego proposed to me." (20:96)

Out of the fire emerged a golden calf, beautiful and red, smooth and shining, the most perfect, pleasing, warm, golden cow. Because of the sand that had touched the Horse of Life, the cow made a lowing sound when the wind blew through it and, some say, it could actually move. The golden image at least seemed to live and breathe, and it was beautiful. As-Samiri told the people,

"This is your god and the god of Musa, but he has forgotten." (20:88)

Once when as-Samiri was a child the angels had opened the heavens for him to see all the way up to the Throne of God.

He had not seen the Throne itself or God, of course, but he had seen one of the mighty angels that support the Throne. This angel has the shape of a cow or bull. From this brief sight he had hidden in his heart a love for cows. To him this cow actually did represent God Almighty and he firmly believed that he knew what Musa ﷺ had forgotten. His sincerity convinced the Children of Israil of his truthfulness. There is a difference between sincerity and truth. Just because someone appears to believe what he says, does not make what he says true. And as-Samiri had at least some idea what was true as evidenced by what he said above.

Now as-Samiri became the leader the people needed to give them the courage to disobey their prophets. They were tired of waiting for Musa ﷺ to reappear. How much they had wanted a little golden god of their own. Now it was theirs and it was perfect in every way. It didn't make any demands on them. It didn't ask them to do things they didn't like. It didn't threaten them or cause them any harm. It didn't set them apart from all the other people. It was simple and visible and not at all confusing. And they missed the bountiful, milk-giving cows of Egypt. The harsh conditions of the Sinai would not support cows, only goats and sheep and camels. With as-Samiri at their head, they were no longer afraid to threaten Harun ﷺ and his staunch followers.

Harun ﷺ was mild mannered and forgiving. He feared being the cause of dissension or division among the people and, without the authority of his brother, Musa ﷺ, he felt he could take no forceful action. The pious people abhor division. Allah says,

"...We enjoined on Ibrahim, Musa, and Isa: Namely that you should remain steadfast in religion, and make no division therein. To those who worship other than Allah, hard is the (way) to which you call them. Allah chooses for Himself those whom He pleases, and guides to Himself those who turn (towards Him)." (42:13)

Some of the believers wanted to fight those who had turned so drastically from the straight path. But Harun ﷺ counseled patience. They would wait for Musa's ﷺ return. There were only twelve thousand true believers who stood firmly behind him, so Harun ﷺ advised them to withdraw and wait. He led the small band of believers across the valley. There they maintained their worship of the one God, whom no one had seen, no one had heard except for Musa ﷺ, but whose signs were clearly all around them.

$$\frac{34}{48}$$

35.

The Heights

Meanwhile, Musa ﷺ had been taken swiftly on the back of the Horse of Life to the mountain where Allah Almighty had first spoken to him so many years ago. This time, however, Jibrail ﷺ did not leave him in the sacred valley at the foot of Mount Tur but rather he took Musa ﷺ all the way to the summit. There on a barren, rocky peak, towering above the other mountains of the Sinai, he left Musa ﷺ alone. He had a narrow hollow in the rock for shelter and a view of the vast sky surrounding him on every side. In this desolate and expansive place he was invited to enter into intimate seclusion with his Lord. Musa ﷺ fell into prostration before the Glory and Majesty of his Lord Almighty and he stayed in that position for thirty days. Musa ﷺ and the mountain were blanketed in a cloud of light out of which the Lord spoke. Together they conversed, the Lord and His servant. They spoke, one to the other, in an almost familiar way; in a way no one has before or since.

Musa ﷺ told his Lord that the people wanted a book of guidance to follow. Allah replied that He would give the Banu Israil a book but He also warned that it was a big responsibility. They would have to commit themselves to keeping the commandments revealed in it. Allah reminded him that He had given His first creation, the Prophet Adam ﷺ, a single commandment. He had told him not to eat the fruit of one tree in a garden of uncountable trees laden with marvelous and delicious fruit. How well did Adam ﷺ do in keeping even that one simple commandment? But the Banu Israil had given their promise and the Gracious Lord accepted.

"and Allah spoke directly to Musa" (4:164)

Allah requested His Prophet to stay on the mountain another ten days in order to complete forty days. Musa ﷺ assented even though he knew that he was breaking his promise to his people. After the forty days of fasting and praying were complete, on a Friday that was also the Day of Arafat, Allah sent for Musa ﷺ to approach close to His Divine Presence. The Archangel Jibrail ﷺ hovered over the mountain and lowered just one of his countless wings. Musa ﷺ, in awe, climbed up using the heavenly jewels that paved its surface, as handholds. No mortal had ever mounted his wing before. The heavenly jewels with which it was studded resembled earthly jewels except their radiance was even more brilliant. Musa ﷺ shielded his eyes with his sleeve and was carried in this way up to the mighty throne of God.

Allah sent down a veil of light to envelop His Prophet and within this light He showed him the Tawrah and filled his heart with all the wisdom he needed to be able to teach his people. He was so close he could hear the many wings of the angels of the Throne and the praises that they sing continuously of their Lord God Most High. He could hear the scratching of the Pen chiseling the letters of the Tawrah on the stone tablets. Musa ﷺ had an experience similar to the Night Journey of the Prophet Muhammad ﷺ only it was conducted in sound rather than sight. In The Quran the sense of hearing is always mentioned before the sense of sight. For example Allah said,

"Fear not surely I am with the both of you (Musa and Harun), Hearing and Seeing." (20:46)

You can hear before you can see, in the spiritual realm as in the material realm. Musa ﷺ was the first to speak to the Almighty directly, not through an intermediary. The Prophet Muhammad was the first to see Allah directly, not through a veil, or a cloud.

When Musa ﷺ was returned to the mountain he was both stunned and in awe. He had the tablets on which the Tawrah was written in his hands, and the words of the Tawrah ringing in his ears. When he had recovered somewhat, however, all he could feel was an overwhelming and all-consuming longing. He wanted to experience closeness to his Lord with every faculty in his possession. Musa ﷺ began to beseech his Lord to let him see His Divine Face. The use of the word 'face' is a metaphor for the incomparable, indescribable, Presence of Allah.

The Lord knew that the earthly realm could not carry such a manifestation but He offered to try to reveal Himself to the mountain opposite Mount Tur. Either way Musa ﷺ felt he would die. If he were shown a vision of his Lord he might die but if he were not shown he felt that he would surely die. Musa ﷺ steadied himself and gazed intently in the direction of the mountain across the way. If the mountain could withstand the majesty of Allah's Divine Magnificence then Musa ﷺ would see Him before his eyes. But the Lord has said,

"Sight cannot reach Him, but He reaches all sight." (6:103)

First Allah, in order to prepare him, sent angels of the sort that have the form of bulls. The pounding of their hooves made the air reverberate with thunder and lightening. They roared at Musa ﷺ as they stampeded past, "You have asked a tremendous thing!" And Musa ﷺ looked and saw the whole sky full of these bellowing bulls and he was terrified and felt that he would surely die. If he had been any other man his heart would have burst from fear and he would certainly have died on the spot.

After the sky had cleared he heard from another direction, a growling roar that steadily increased. Allah sent a second sort of angel that has the form of a lion. Their crimson mouths were open, baring long and fearsome teeth and their growls were deep and resounding. They roared, "La ilaha illa Allah, There is no God but Allah. You can hardly bear to see us. How will you see the Lord?" And Musa ﷺ fell to the ground sickened and hiding his eyes.

After the sky had quieted down a second time, he heard a new sound as a third group of angels descended before him. They were made in the form of giant falcons. Their wings swept the entire horizon and they flapped and shrieked the high-pitched screech of the earthly falcon, only many magnitudes louder. Their wings stirred up cyclones in the air and the noise and tumult was almost heart stopping. Their warning pierced Musa's ﷺ ears until he could neither hear nor think anything else. "How can you bear us?" they shrieked.

After a while the sky became quiet again. Musa ﷺ turned his head in the fourth direction from which came a terrible sound of feet pounding the sky like relentless drums. It was the fourth sort of angel made in the form of massive, muscular, men. The solemn sound of these gigantic strongmen drummed in Musa's ﷺ ears and was more fearful and terrible than all the others combined. These angels thundered at Musa ﷺ as they stomped past, "How dare you ask for such a thing?"

These were troops of angels of the four kinds that carry the Throne of God. Four angels carry the majestic Throne of the Almighty, the symbol of His Dominion; one angel supports each corner. These angels have the form of a bull, a lion, a falcon and a man. It is said that the individual angels change every day. Another angel of the same form takes their place. No angel ever does this job a second time ever again for all of eternity. It is also said that the Throne is such a wonder of jewels and precious things that there is no possibility that four angels, regardless of their size or strength, could lift it even for a second. It is, in actuality, the Throne that supports the angels.

Musa's ﷺ love and determination were not diminished in the least. He roused himself one more time and fixed his eyes on the neighboring mountain. Allah Almighty released one tiny portion of the light from His Face – maybe the amount that could pass through the eye of a needle or maybe less. It is said that Allah Almighty sent one ray of His light and that He veiled that ray with seventy thousand veils. The solid, stony mountain shattered like a delicate tea glass and crashed to the ground. Musa's ﷺ consciousness shattered as well and he fell, senseless, face down upon the ground.

Allah says in The Quran,

"Had We caused this Quran to descend upon a mountain, verily, you (Muhammad) would have seen it humble itself and break apart for fear of Allah. Such are the parables that We present to men that they may reflect." (59:21)

Musa ﷺ remained in prostration like this for three days. Some say that he died on the top of the mountain and that he awoke only when Allah gave him new life three days later. The Prophet Muhammad ﷺ said that on the Day of Resurrection he will lift his head and he will see Musa ﷺ clinging to the Throne of God. At that time he will not know if Musa ﷺ was resurrected ahead of him or not. It is possible, he said, that Musa ﷺ had already died on Mount Tur and been resurrected then. Since we are promised only one death, Musa ﷺ like Ilyas ﷺ, and Idris ﷺ might have been taken still living into heaven to await the Judgment Day.

Others say that Musa ﷺ fainted and remained unconscious for some time before the angel Jibrail ﷺ was sent to revive him. In any case when he awoke his face had been permanently altered. The Divine Light that he had witnessed had permeated his own face. No one could look directly at him any longer. Those with strong faith would go blind if they saw him, and those with weaker faith would die instantly.

Musa ﷺ humbled himself before the Majesty of his Lord. Allah the Generous had given all he was able to receive. He was at peace and satisfied. However he now had another problem. How would he be able to carry out his duties of leading and teaching if no one could look at his face without dying? Allah told Musa ﷺ to take some of the worn-out clothes of a man who although tested by poverty had remained patient, or the clothes of a scholar who had studied for the sole purpose of achieving nearness to Allah. He should make himself a turban and draw the end of it over his face as a veil. This would prevent the light shining from his face from either burning or blinding those who saw him. From that time on, no man saw Musa ﷺ except through the layers of a veil. Even so it is said that the light from his face shone so brightly that it illuminated a tiny ant a parsang (6 km) away.

But the wife of Musa ﷺ could not bear to be without the sight of her beloved husband. She begged and pleaded with him to let her see his face. He warned her of the consequences. But, just as he had not been afraid to lose his life in order to see the face of his Lord, so Saffura's ﷺ love impelled her to insist. Finally he unveiled himself in front of her. In a burst of love, she died. Musa ﷺ pleaded with his Lord to revive her. As soon as she was recovered she begged again to see his face. Again he revealed himself. Again she expired. Three times she saw him and three times she endured the pangs of death, so great was her love of the light of her Lord.

The mountain on which Allah Almighty had revealed His Light had crumbled to dust except for seven large pieces. Three pieces flew to Mecca the Ennobled. One of these became Jabal Nur, also called Hira, where the Prophet ﷺ used to go for retreat and on which he received the first revelation of The Quran. The second piece became Jabal Thawr where the Prophet ﷺ hid in the cave with AbuBakr as-Siddiq ﷺ during their escape to Madina. The third piece became the mountain called Thabir.

Three of the pieces also flew to Madina the Enlightened. One of these became Jabal Uhud, the mountain that gave shelter to the Prophet ﷺ when he was wounded and his life threatened during the second big battle of Islam. The Prophet ﷺ said about this mountain, "It is from us and we are from it". It is believed that an entrance to Heaven lies beneath it. Two other pieces became the mountains of Warqan and Radwa. The seventh piece was catapulted into the sky between heaven and earth where it will continue to orbit until Judgment Day.

משה

35/48

36.

Righteous Anger

Before he descended the mountain Allah Almighty showed Musa ﷺ what his people had been doing since he had left them. Musa ﷺ saw them reflected in the air, as we would see a reflection in water. They were bowing to a statue of a golden cow. They were drinking and dancing and acting in disgraceful and lewd ways. Musa ﷺ in anguish cried out to his Lord. How could He have allowed His people to do such things? Allah answered him,

"We have tried your people in your absence, and as-Samiri has misled them." (20:85)

Musa ﷺ was filled with righteous anger. He was furious with the Banu Israil for being so weak and faithless. But he was willing to make excuses for them to his Lord, saying "O my Lord, if You had not tempted and tested them they would not have sinned." But of course this is the purpose of the world and its creation, to test and to try with good and with evil, so that each soul can learn the lessons it requires in order to return, "pleased and well-pleasing" to its Creator. (89:28)

No Prophet has ever, before or since, talked to his Lord with such familiarity. Musa ﷺ spoke his heart openly because his heart was pure. All that was contained within it was love for Allah. His only thought was to serve his Lord and complete his mission. The manner in which he acted was according to the Divine name in whose image he had been created. It was his nature to be fierce in his righteousness and forthright in speaking

"Musa threw down the tablets" (7:150) and most of the words flew back to Heaven

his heart.

The angels helped Musa ﷺ carry the tablets of the Word of Allah down the mountain. They were too heavy for a man to carry. Some say there were two Tablets, some say nine and some even say forty. At the base he found in front of him the scene that Allah had shown him in the vision on the mountain, only it was much worse in actuality. The Banu Israil, the descendants of prophets, the ones for whom God had parted the sea and destroyed the pharaoh, the ones God Almighty had chosen for Himself, were circling a golden statue, praising it and worshiping it as if it were God.

Musa ﷺ had left the Divine Presence to return to them, to be their teacher and leader. He had asked his Lord, on their behalf, for favors and was bringing them all they had asked for. He had in his hands the Book and the Law, which they had solemnly sworn to obey. The first two commandments it contained, however, they had already broken. He had been upset on the mountain. He had even blamed the Almighty for what had happened. But now that he saw it before his very eyes, it was too horrendous a sight for him to support.

Without saying a word Musa ﷺ took up the Tablets, which up to that point he had not even been able to carry, and in his mighty disgust dashed them to the ground. His weak people were unfit for the trust that had been placed upon them. They could not carry the great gift of the Law. The Tablets fell to the ground and, with a thunderous noise, shattered into many pieces.

Today in much of the Muslim world when someone breaks a glass by mistake those around him say, "May it take away evil". There is something about the sound of breaking that also breaks the moment and awakens awareness. In this case the Banu Israil were stunned to silence. Looking around them they must have cried in dismay, "What have we done?" The atmosphere of orgiastic oblivion shattered into a thousand pieces and the people awoke to their real selves and to terrible remorse and repentance.

When the tablets broke it is said that most of the words of the Tawrah flew back to heaven. Only one seventh of the words of the original Tawrah remained on two tablets and even these may have been broken. What a great loss this was to mankind. But like everything else it was according to the plan of the Creator. There is a Hadith in which the Prophet Muhammad ﷺ related a story of the meeting in Heaven of Adam ﷺ and Musa ﷺ. Musa ﷺ reproached Adam ﷺ for disobeying the Lord and bringing about the expulsion of mankind from Paradise. Muhammad ﷺ said that Adam ﷺ won the dispute by replying, "How can you blame me for what was decreed for me from before I was even created?" In just this way the Tawrah must have been intended to be only partly written, with the larger part to be passed unwritten from master to disciple.

Musa ﷺ approached his brother Harun ﷺ. In his distress and disappointment he grabbed his brother by the beard and shouted at him for not having been able to keep the believers on the straight path. Why didn't you come find me, why didn't you do something, he cried in agony to his brother? But Harun ﷺ pleaded with him to understand that he had not been strong enough.

Harun ﷺ and twelve thousand of the believers had tried to reason with the people. Some of the men wanted to fight and destroy the calf but Harun ﷺ had counseled patience. Men of God hate anything that causes division among the people and avoid it at all costs. They did everything in their power, except resort to violence, to dissuade their people from following as-Samiri and worshipping the calf. Finally, afraid for their own lives, because they were heavily outnumbered, they retreated to a distant place. There they continued to worship the One God and to wait for the return of Musa ﷺ.

This, however, was not the time or place for patience. The people had crossed all limits. They needed to be reined in for their own good, in fact, for their very salvation. Patience and gentleness are not the remedies for every illness. Sometimes righteous anger, that is anger on behalf of the Truth, followed by punishment is the only means of stopping destructive behavior. Musa ﷺ was upset with his brother for what he first saw as betrayal and disobedience. The Jews, in their books, actually accuse their Prophet Harun ﷺ of aiding as-Samiri in establishing the golden idol. But without doubt, no prophet of God could fall to such depths. The Quran clearly states,

"And when Musa returned to his people, angry and sad, he said: Evil is what you did after I left. Would you hasten on the commandment of your Lord? He cast down the tablets, and he seized his brother by the head, dragging him towards him. He [Harun] said: Son of my mother! Surely, the people judged me weak and almost killed me. Do not make my enemies to triumph over me and place me not among the evildoers. He [Musa] said: My Lord, have mercy on me and on my brother; bring us into Your Mercy, You are the Most Merciful of all those who show mercy." (7: 150-151)

The majority of the people on seeing the return and the anger of their prophet began to feel ashamed of their actions. They all pointed to as-Samiri as the one who had misled them. They explained that they had only obeyed him because he said he knew the calf was actually the god of Musa ﷺ and they were too weak to object. Now they all pointed to as-Samiri as the one who had led them astray as if they had not made the choice to follow him.

How can we understand this part of the story? How was it possible for a people, so favored and so honored, to disregard all the miraculous events that had just occurred for their benefit and turn to such a pathetically ignorant practice? We are obligated to ask this question for we have been told that before our time is over, we too, will find ourselves committing the same offense.

Allah says:

"Man is made of haste. I shall show you My signs, but

ask me not to hasten." (21:37)

Everything has its place and its time. You cannot bring it sooner and it cannot be delayed. This is Allah's timing and either you submit to it willingly and happily, or unwillingly and with pain. If they had been patient everything would have come to them in its proper time. Musa ﷺ had endured with patience many years of trials; he had been carefully prepared by his Lord. The majority of the Banu Israil had hardly begun their training. While Musa ﷺ was fasting and praying for forty days, the people were too impatient to wait or follow him. They miscounted the days, gave up hope and stopped obeying. Allah says He loves the ones who are patient and enduring. Their lack of resolve and patience was what produced the calf.

Allah also says:

"Man prays for evil as he prays for good; for Man was ever hasty. (17: 11)

Haste implies the inexorable passing of time, which is the defining dimension of this temporal world. Time, with the world in tow, is rushing away and the more you run after it, the more it rushes ahead of you. Only the Hereafter is eternal, abiding. Physical man, like the physical world, is made of haste; he is chained to time, always moving on regardless if it is to good or to evil.

After the Banu Israil had crossed the sea and been saved from Pharaoh, Musa ﷺ had settled them under the authority of his brother, Harun ﷺ, and rushed to his appointment with his Lord on the mountain in Sinai. Allah Almighty asked his Prophet why he had rushed to leave his people and he replied that his only intention had been to seek the pleasure of his Lord. Allah accepted this sincere answer from His prophet. On descending the mountain and finding his people gone so astray, Musa ﷺ asked them the same question: Why did you rush?

"Would you hasten on the commandment of your Lord?" (7:150)

It is the same question but with two different answers.

"Whoever desires that which hastens away (the transitory life), We hasten it on for him, what We will for whom We want. And in the end We have provided Hell for them, disgraced and rejected. And whoever desires the Hereafter...their effort finds favor with their Lord." (17:18-19)

The Arabic word for 'calf' and the word for 'haste' are etymologically related; they derive from the same three letter root – 'ajl. The calf represents time, the temporal and the temporary. The Banu Israil became distracted by concerns for the things of this world. Whether out of fear or greed, weakness or arrogance, they sought the solution for their problems from what was available at hand in the world rather than depending on the One who created it. Making haste for the world results in suffering and punishment. Making haste for the Hereafter results in contentment and success. The Banu Israil chose this transitory life while Musa ﷺ was calling them to choose eternity.

Musa ﷺ picked up the tablets that he had thrown on the ground. It is said that six sevenths of the words had flown back to Heaven. The pieces that remained Musa ﷺ collected. What was to be done with the sinning people? Musa ﷺ had more than just the pieces of the Tawrah to pick up and put back together.

As-Samiri was sentenced to wander the world, crying, "Touch me not," like a leper. He was expelled from the community of believers. No one would speak to him. No one would offer him shelter or hospitality. No one would give him a smile or a kind word. Like Adam's ﷺ son, Qabil, who killed his brother Habil ﷺ, he was banished from human company and forced to wander the world alone, in misery and sorrow, until his death. Then at that time he would face the final judgment of his Lord.

Once again, as with Qarun, we have an example of a man who was given great gifts from God that only served to encourage him in following shaytan into envy and rebellion. As-Samiri was not given material wealth and temporal authority like Qarun, rather he was given significant spiritual gifts. As-Samiri had been saved from Pharaoh, and nursed on the wing of the Archangel Jibrail ﷺ. He had been favored with spiritual vision and insight. These had only served to make him proud and incapable of submitting to those with even greater understanding than his own. Sometimes it is said, 'the only thing worse than no knowledge at all, is a little bit of knowledge". A true knower must know first of all, that in comparison to the oceans of Divine Knowledge, whatever he knows is at most just a tiny drop. Secondly he must know that above every knower there is always someone who knows more.

משה

36/48

37.

Hearts Of Gold

The people made excuses for themselves. They had only followed as-Samiri because he had said that he possessed knowledge and that the calf represented the real god of Musa ﷺ. Their faith was not strong and they didn't want to cause trouble. They all went along with what everyone else was doing.

Musa ﷺ ordered that the golden calf be burned and that its ashes be thrown in the sea. Since it is difficult to reduce metal to ash some people say that they chipped away at the statue until only a heap of metal filings remained and these they threw into the sea.

Most of the people began to feel great remorse for what they had done once they saw the disgust and anger on the face of their prophet. They had disobeyed and fallen short again. Musa ﷺ told them that they must try to gain the forgiveness of their Lord because the punishment for what they had done was death. He chose seventy men whom he judged to be the purest and best among them, some from each of the twelve tribes. He instructed them to purify themselves, to fast and to pray, and to prepare to petition their Lord on behalf of their people.

The seventy men followed the instructions of their prophet sincerely. They cleansed themselves and they fasted all day until the hour past sundown. At this time they ate and drank, after which they began their fast again immediately. This was the fasting regimen ordained for the Banu Israil. They prayed fifty prayers every day. And they shouldered their responsibility with apparent sincerity. They begged to go up the mountain

"We hear and we rebel." (2:93) The Banu Israil atone for their sin.

with Musa ﷺ to plead with the Lord and to hear His commands with their own ears.

After some days of preparation, Musa ﷺ led them to the foot of Mt. Sinai and together they climbed to the summit, to the spot where Musa ﷺ had an appointment with his Lord. A cloud of light settled around the prophet. Allah Almighty invited the seventy to come closer until they also entered into the cloud of light. Then they heard the awesome sound of Musa ﷺ in conversation with Allah Almighty. They heard the Lord tell Musa ﷺ what was permitted and what was prohibited. They heard so many restrictions and rules that instead of confirming their faith it made them rebellious and obstinate. They then asked to also be made prophets and said

"O Musa, we will never believe in you until we see God openly." (2:55)

In answer to this statement, the seventy men heard a sound like a blast, a bone-rattling clap of thunder. Lightening flashed around them. It was as if the sky were being torn apart and the stars were bursting on the ground all around them. They could not stand up under the fear that gripped them. Their knees buckled, their eyes rolled back in their heads and they were seized by powerful trembling. Death took them by surprise. Their hearts stopped beating and they fell to the ground. All seventy of Israil's finest lay dead on top of the mountain.

When Allah Almighty had finished addressing Musa ﷺ and Musa ﷺ was filled with love and longing for his Lord, the cloud was lifted away. To his horror, Musa ﷺ saw before him the best of his nation lying dead on the ground. He was grief-stricken. The hope of his people, his supporters and his chiefs, those who were the foundation on which he hoped to build a community of believers, lay dead.

How was he to lay the groundwork for a nation, and to follow his Lord's instruction if those on whom he depended were all dead? And what would their families and their tribes say when they were told of their deaths? Surely those who remained at the foot of the mountain would blame him for the deaths of their kinsmen. They would never accept his leadership again. He had enough trouble getting them to listen in the first place. Now he cried out to his Lord to undo the terrible thing that had been done, to bring the seventy back to life.

But Allah knew what His Prophet did not know. Allah knows what is hidden in the hearts of men. These seventy men, chosen by Musa ﷺ for their sincerity and purity, had hidden deep in their hearts a love for a golden calf. Not one of them was truly pure. These men had withdrawn from the outward actions of their people. They had not physically worshiped the calf, nor danced, nor sung, nor cavorted around it. They were truly the best of the people but still Allah Almighty found in their hearts traces of love for something other than Him.

"And the calf was made to sink into their hearts because of their refusal to acknowledge the Truth. Say: Evil is that which your belief commands you, if you are believers." (2:93)

Idol worship is not only the act of stupid, depraved humans who make a statue and then pretend it is God. Idol worship describes reverence for anything other than the Creator. Anything at all, whether good or bad, can be an idol: our desires, personal opinions, noble values, or ideologies - artistic, scientific, or political. Even religious practices, or spiritual states, can become idols. If we created them and adhere to them religiously they replace God. If our aim is to please anyone or anything other than God in any of the smallest of our actions or intentions, we can be judged as idol worshipers. Even our prayer can be an idol if we created it and it pleases us. The ritual Muslim prayer is a formula that derives solely from God's own words. We can only truly worship God by means of God.

Musa ﷺ had also asked to see the Face of his Lord and had been brought near death. But he had asked out of longing and love. He had been willing and content to die if that was the consequence. He had no other intention in his heart than to be near the one he loved. The seventy righteous men had asked in pride and rebellion. They had said,

"We hear and we rebel." (2:93)

They wanted to be prophets. They wanted to be important, or respected, or holy. They wanted gifts of inspiration, grace or knowledge. They also worshipped haste. They insisted that they be shown the face of the Lord before they were ready or had been chosen. Musa ﷺ only wanted his Lord's pleasure.

The Lord Most High, to please His faithful servant, sent Jibrail ﷺ to blow the souls of the seventy back into their bodies. They began to cough and sputter. In different stages of awakening they watched each other revive. They were deeply repentant. They had asked for more than they had the right. Shamed and humbled, they were informed that Allah did not accept their repentance on behalf of their nation.

What now was the punishment of the Banu Israil who had betrayed the trust of their prophet and their Lord? The punishments at that time were much more severe than they are now. The punishment for forsaking the worship of the Lord was no less than death. Allah Almighty decreed that the twelve thousand who had not actually worshiped the calf were to execute the others who had. Everyone accepted this punishment as fair, both the ones who had worshipped the cow and the ones who had not.

The men who had participated in the worship of the calf now hoped for forgiveness and a life of eternal bliss after their death. They submitted willingly to be executed. The twelve thousand took up their swords. The condemned fell to their knees in long lines that stretched along the sandy valley floor. They wrapped themselves in their cloaks and waited without crying or struggling. Allah sent a dense fog that covered everyone so that the ones wielding the swords of justice did not have to look at the faces of those they executed. They swung their swords until the ground ran with blood.

Musa ﷺ, Harun ﷺ, the women, children, and young boys stood to one side and prayed with all their hearts for the forgiveness of their nation. After many hours the fog lifted. Seventy thousand men lay dead on the ground. Those who remained were forgiven and the ones who lay dead were received as martyrs by the angels of heaven. This was in strict fulfillment of the Law given to the Banu Israil.

Musa ﷺ and Harun ﷺ mourned the deaths of their companions. There were so many dead that there were hardly enough men left to bury them. How could they establish the rule of God's Law on earth with so few to follow them? "You are not content with My Justice?" asked Allah. "Those who repented, and accepted their punishment, are forgiven and are now entering Paradise. Those who executed them will, in time, certainly enter Paradise because they obeyed My command. Could either of you wish anything better than this for your people?" And Musa ﷺ and Harun ﷺ could find no argument with the perfection of God's Justice.

38.

Tablets And Tawrah

Some say that Musa ﷺ went back up the mountain a third time and Allah replaced the broken Tablets. Others say that the broken ones were collected and restored. In any case Musa ﷺ taught Harun ﷺ what had been taught to him and together they set about educating the people who remained about the contents and meanings of the Tawrah that had been entrusted to them.

"And We wrote for him, upon the tablets, the lesson to be drawn from all things and the explanation of all things…" (7:145)

It is said that the original Tablets were made of heavenly gemstones: the Jews say blue sapphire and the Muslims say green emerald. They were carved by God's Hand of Power in such a way, that they could be read from any side, up or down, and they still appeared correctly, almost as if the words floated freely inside the stone itself. But after they were broken, they were replaced by regular, earthly stone.

It is said that there were two Tablets, or nine or even forty. They were inscribed with the Ten Commandments but between the lines were written three hundred and sixty-five principles, as many as the days of the year, and two hundred and forty-seven prohibitions, as many as the parts of the body that can be disobedient. Some say that the original Tawrah consisted of eight hundred words. Some say it consisted of one hundred and fourteen thousand words. Some say it consisted of only

"We wrote for him upon the tablets the lesson to be drawn from all things" (7:145)

what is known as the Ten Commandments. Some say that after the Tablets were broken most of the words flew back to Heaven. The evidence used for this in the classical literature is the verse above. Allah states that He wrote the Tawrah as an explanation of all things in detail. But when the Tawrah is described after its creation it is only said to be a guidance and a mercy.

The Jews say today that the Tawrah consists of five books, called the Books of Musa ﷺ: Genesis, Exodus, Leviticus, Numbers, and Deuteronomy. They believe these constitute the original Tawrah, exactly as it was received by Musa ﷺ. They say that the first copy of the Tawrah was written down by Musa ﷺ himself on a scroll of leather. The Christians call these same five books, the Pentateuch, the first five books of the Old Testament. The Muslims respect the Tawrah and take wisdom from it but have evidence to believe that some of the original was destroyed and lost and that what is left may have been severely altered over the many millennia since it was revealed.

"Say: Who revealed the Book which Musa brought, a light and a guidance for mankind, which you have put on parchment which you show, but you hide much…" (6:91)

The Prophet Muhammad ﷺ said, when asked about the scriptures of the Jews and Christians, "Do not believe the People of the Book, nor disbelieve, but say: We believe in Allah and whatever He revealed to us and whatever He revealed to you." Because if you dismiss all of it, you may be dismissing the Word of God and if you accept all of it, you may be accepting what is wrong. Keep to the latest most accurate of the scriptures, The Holy Quran.

The Banu Israil recognize, in actuality, two Tawrah. One they call the written Tawrah, which was the one inscribed on the Tablets. The other they call the oral Tawrah, which was the one placed in the heart of Musa ﷺ and passed by word of mouth from one generation to the next. This second Tawrah was eventually written down, because it was feared that it was being forgotten, and it now forms what is known as the Mishna, a part of the Talmud.

In a holy Hadith the Prophet Muhammad ﷺ said: "The Lord gave to Musa ﷺ the Tablets of the Tawrah and upon them was written: I am the Lord, Allah. Attribute no partners to Me, for those who attribute partners to Me I will burn in the fires of Hell. Give thanks to Me, and honor your father and mother. Do not swear falsely by My Name and envy no one, for envy is the enemy of My bounty. Be content with what I have given you, for whoever is not content with what he is given is not one of My servants. Give your heart to none but to Me alone and keep far from pride. Love your brother as you love yourself and keep the Sabbath."

The list of the Ten Commandments differs between the Jews and the Christians slightly in language and in numbering but in content they are much the same. This is one rendering:

1. I am the Lord your God, who brought you out of the land of Egypt, out of slavery. You shall have no god but Me. 2. You shall make no idols or graven images. 3. You shall not take the name of the Lord your God in vain. 4. Remember the Sabbath day and keep it holy. 5. Honor your father and your mother. 6. Do not murder. 7. Do not commit adultery. 8. Do not steal. 9. Do not testify falsely. 10. Do not envy.

It is interesting to note that, over his lifetime the Banu Israil falsely accused their prophet of violating almost every single one of these commandments. Commandments 1 and 2: as-Samiri claimed that the golden calf was the god of Musa ﷺ and the people believed him. In fact the Jews to this day accuse Harun ﷺ of having helped to erect the idol. Commandment 3: They accused Musa ﷺ of not keeping his sacred promise to return to them after thirty days. Commandment 5: He had, in their view, betrayed the Pharaoh who had been a foster father to him. Commandment 6: They accused him of murdering the Egyptian slave driver although it had been an accident. Commandment 7: Qarun accused him of adultery. Commandments 8 and 9: When he ordered the earth to consume Qarun, his people said that he wanted to steal his treasures and was condemning him unjustly. Commandment 10: They said he was jealous of the love the people felt for his brother Harun ﷺ.

The only commandment they did not accuse him of breaking was that of keeping the Sabbath. The Banu Israil, on the other hand, did actually break all of the commandments at least once during the lifetime of the Prophet Musa ﷺ.

In addition to these commandments, the Banu Israil were required to pray fifty times each day and each prayer had to be performed in congregation within their place of worship. To cleanse themselves for prayer they had to wash seven times and any clothing that was soiled had to be cut away, it could not be washed. Fasting was required of them six months out of the year and they only had one hour in which to break their fast each evening. The punishment for most major sins was death.

Muslims today only need to wash for prayer once and can clean their soiled clothes with water. They can pray in any place they find themselves; the whole world is a temple for the nation of Muhammad ﷺ. Fasting is required only one month out of the year and they may eat and drink from sunset to sunrise. Even the penalties for most sins are less severe. Just by asking for forgiveness, Allah in all His abundant Mercy, forgives us.

When the Prophet Muhammad ﷺ was brought to visit the Seven Heavens on the Night Journey he met many of the earlier prophets. In the Fifth Heaven he met Harun ﷺ who he described as being very beautiful. In the Sixth Heaven he met Musa ﷺ who greeted him as a brother and cried when they parted. On his return journey, after leaving the Divine Presence, Musa ﷺ asked him how many daily prayers their Lord had assigned to the Muslim people. The Prophet Muhammad ﷺ answered that he had been given fifty, just as Musa ﷺ had been given before him. Musa ﷺ said: "That is too heavy for your people, as it was for mine. Go back to your Lord while you still can, and plead with Him to lessen the number."

The Prophet Muhammad ﷺ went back and Allah Almighty reduced the number of prayers to forty. Still when he passed through the sixth heaven Musa ﷺ advised him to return a second time and then a third, forth and fifth, until the number of prayers had been reduced to five. Musa ﷺ again counseled Muhammad ﷺ to ask for less but the Prophet ﷺ was too shy to petition his Lord a sixth time. Surely all Muslims have Musa ﷺ to thank for the fact that we have only five daily prayers and that, in the Divine Presence, they are still counted as fifty. Musa ﷺ was well familiar with the weakness of people and that even these five prayers can seem like a heavy burden.

The Children of Israil did not find these rules and regulations easy to accept. They had never had to do these things before. These laws invaded every aspect of the people's lives. Again they rebelled. The Banu Israil refused to bow their heads to their Creator or submit to His Almighty Law. In the recent past they had raised their heads too high and asked to hear the Lord and then see the Lord. For this they had actually died. But the ego of man is tough and does not submit without a fight. Truly the Banu Israil were fighters by nature, and strong.

Allah Almighty sent His angels to tear the mountain of Sinai, Mount Tur, up out of the ground by it roots as if it were a great tree. The angels, on the command of their Lord, held this mountain above the heads of the believers. The sky darkened and the Banu Israil saw the unmistakable, craggy shape of the mountain on which their Prophet ﷺ had spent months in the company of God Almighty, looming over them and threatening to crush them. They fell to the ground in fear and in supplication. Finally they submitted, at least temporarily, to the Lord of all the Worlds.

$\dfrac{38}{48}$

39.

Tabut And Tabernacle

The Banu Israil say that Musa ﷺ went three times to the top of Jabal Tur. The first time he stayed for forty days in prostration on the rocky ground, his face pressed into the earth. The second time he sat or kneeled in prayer to his Lord for forty days. The third time he stood in prayer for forty days until the Tablets of the Book were given to him.

After he smashed the Tablets on the ground because his people had betrayed their trust he picked up the pieces that remained and put them in a box called the Tabut in Arabic. The Muslims say that either there were two Tablets that remained unbroken or that Musa ﷺ ascended the mountain again and received two new Tablets that replaced the broken ones. In any case he was instructed by Allah to build a box in which to carry the Tablets.

Allah Almighty was very specific about the size and dimensions of this box called 'Tebah' in Hebrew and refered to as 'The Ark of the Covenant" in English. According to the Tawrah, it was to be made of acacia wood, two and a half meters long, one and a half meters wide and one and a half meters high. The whole box was then to be plated with solid gold, inside and out. The lid of the box was to have a rim like a crown. On the top, images of two angels, carved from solid gold, were to be placed facing each other, their wings wrapped around their bodies and then touching. The box had rings on each side through which golden poles were inserted so it could be carried, as a litter is carried.

At night when they stopped they set up the Tabernacle. "In it is the Sakina from your Lord." (2:248)

The Muslims say that the box was wood and made just like the little coffin, tabut, in which the baby Musa ﷺ was placed into the river. The Tablets of the Law were so heavy and majestic that Musa ﷺ had not been able to carry them down from the mountain. Rather Allah had sent angels to transport the Tablets. The Tabut was placed on a wagon and drawn by a team of oxen aided by the invisible support of angels. Men could not carry it. Probably the golden angels on the top are representations of the real angels that supported the Tabut. It seems strange that the God, who so forcefully forbade His servants from worshipping images, just after sentencing them to death for worshipping a golden cow, would have demanded they put golden figures on the holiest relic in the new religion. But the Jews say that God, recognizing the weakness of the people, granted them the golden figures they so desired, but in the appropriate place. Only God knows the truth.

Inside the Tabut they put the two unbroken Tablets of the Tawrah, or the many pieces of the broken Tablets. Eventually they also put inside, the relics of the two prophets, Musa ﷺ and Harun ﷺ: their robes, the staff of Harun ﷺ, shoes and a jar of 'manna', the heavenly food that supported the believers in the desert. The transforming staff of Musa ﷺ did not remain among the people after his death. It was taken back into Heaven.

Also associated with the Tabut was the Sakina, a divine presence or spiritual emanation that was connected to the physical ark. Sayyidina Ali ﷜ described the Sakina as "a sweet breeze whose face is like the face of a human." It brings with it an intense feeling of peace and security. The Muslim armies at the time of the Prophet ﷺ were comforted by the Sakina. Its name in both Arabic and Hebrew derives from the three consonant root, meaning to dwell. It is the in-dwelling of God, the inner sanctuary of the Divine Presence, as when Allah says, "Neither My heavens nor My earth can contain Me. Only the heart of My believing servant can contain Me." (Hadith Qudsi)

At the time of Musa ﷺ the Sakina was connected particularly to the Tabut, where it would descend like a cloud from which the Voice of God would be heard. At the time of Muhammad ﷺ it descended on the believers and filled their hearts. However, there is a Hadith that relates that one companion was riding in the desert. He stopped to pray and was reciting Surat Al Kahf when a cloud descended and settled around him. His horse would have bolted if it had not been securely tied. The next morning the man questioned the Prophet ﷺ who said it was the Sakina, which had come to listen to The Quran being recited.

"And their messenger said to them: Verily! The sign of his kingdom is that there shall come to you At-Tabut wherein is the Sakina from your Lord and a remnant of that which Moses and Harun left behind, carried by angels." (2:248)

This Tabut is also called 'The Ark of the Covenant": Ark, because like Noah's ark, it carried a precious cargo safely through the perils of this world; Covenant, because the Tablets were a Divine law that the Banu Israil had agreed, made a covenant with God, to live by and uphold.

The Tabut became for the Banu Israil the center of their religious practice. When Allah wanted to speak to His Prophet ﷺ from then on, He spoke from a cloud that descended on the top of the Tabut. As they journeyed the Tabut was carried out in front of the people. It preceded them in battle and protected them. When the Tabut was with them, the believers could not be defeated nor could they fall into harm. As they journeyed through the Sinai the Banu Israil carried the Tabut with them.

At night when they stopped, before they set up their tents, they set up the Tabernacle. The Tabernacle was a rectangular enclosure, like a fence whose walls were made of cloth tied to poles. In the center of this enclosure was a tent whose walls were of many colored blankets of goat hair and whose roof was made out of the skins of a ram. Both the tent and its surrounding fence were always oriented towards the East. The tent was divided on the inside into two parts by a curtain. The outer room was called

'The Holy Place' and it contained a table, a standing oil lamp and an altar for burning incense. Behind the curtain was a cube shaped inner space called 'The Holy of Holies'. It was similar in shape and orientation to the Ka'aba in Mecca. Its dimensions were ten cubits on each side, the same height that Musa ﷺ was supposed to be. This was the room within which the Tabut was set, covered with a special linen cloth. The Tabut was covered both for its own protection and for the protection of the people, who might die if exposed to its unmitigated glory.

Allah inspired Musa ﷺ to make Harun ﷺ the keeper of the Tabut. Only he and his male descendents had permission to touch the items in or around the Tabut. The leaders of the other tribes felt jealous and objected to the choice of Harun ﷺ. They wanted the honor of being the keeper of the Holy of Holies for themselves. They felt that Musa ﷺ had unfairly favored his own tribe and his own brother above the others.

So Musa ﷺ was inspired to have each of the leaders of each of the tribes place his staff inside the Tabernacle for the night. In the morning they would all see which one Allah would choose. They did this and in the morning when they opened the Tabernacle they found that the staff of Harun ﷺ, a dry branch of almond wood, had sprouted green leaves and even, some say, ripe fruit. The choice was clear. From that time on only the male descendants of Harun ﷺ could see or touch the Tabut itself or its contents. Anyone else would simply die. Two sons of Harun ﷺ actually did die as a result of making a mistake in the sacred ritual. They were incinerated on the spot. All the male descendants of Harun ﷺ are known as Cohans and only from them are the high priests chosen. Oddly enough the descendants of Musa ﷺ were not distinguished from others of their tribe.

The Tabut stayed with the Banu Israil until their faith faltered. Then it was captured by their enemies who, finding it too dangerous to keep, sent it back. Its discovery served as a sign of the kingship of Saul during the time of the Prophet Samuel ﷺ. The Banu Israil continued to benefit from its blessed presence until the final destruction of the Temple of Sulayman in 586 BCE. It was either captured or hidden at that time and its whereabouts became the subject of speculation and legend. Muslims say that it was divinely protected and will reappear with Al-Mahdi ﷺ at the End of Days. It will precede him in battle, the angels carrying it, and he will defeat all unbelievers.

The Sakina stayed with the Tabut until its disappearance. The Bible (Jeremiah 3:16) says that at some point in the future no one among the Believers will even remember or inquire about the Ark of the Covenant. At that time, so the Rabbis interpret, the Sakina will dwell in the hearts of the people as if their hearts had become the Tabut itself. Referring to the community of the Prophet Muhammad ﷺ, The Quran states,

"It is He Who sent the Sakina to the hearts of the believers that they might add faith to their faith. Allah's are the hosts of Heaven and Earth and Allah is Knower, Wise." (48:4)

משה

39/48

40.

A Giant Mistake

After all these miraculous events and terrible consequences, the believers regrouped. They received their first order from their Lord. They were to sharpen their swords, fletch their arrows and prepare for war. Allah Almighty ordered them to cross the Jordan River and take the city of Jericho from the tyrants who occupied it. Allah was giving the beautiful Jordan valley to the Banu Israil as their homeland. All they had to do was trust in Him Almighty and do their best. They had the two prophets of the Lord with them and also the Ark of the Covenant to steady their fears.

Musa ﷺ and Harun ﷺ consulted with the elders of all the tribes and decided to send one trustworthy man from each of the twelve tribes to scout out the situation across the river. The twelve men would cross the river under cover of darkness and mingle with the people to see what kind of defenses they had and how big a fighting force. Among the twelve was Yusha ﷺ (Joshua) Musa's ﷺ close companion and Kilab (Caleb), his brother-in-law.

When the sun rose the scouts were astounded by what they saw: the city of Jericho was surrounded by high walls and strong fortifications. The people who lived there were men of gigantic stature and enormous strength. The scouts felt as small as insects and knew that to those people they probably actually looked like nothing more than grasshoppers.

It is said that one of the giants was particularly enormous and cranky. His name was Uj son of Unq. He had been born to one of the daughters of the Prophet Adam ﷺ and had been

"They said: O Musa! We will never enter" (5:24)

angry and rebellious even as a boy. At the time of Noah ﷺ he was still alive and living with his wife in the mountains. He had a voracious appetite. He would eat any and every thing he came across and his hunger was never satisfied. Sometimes he worked for the people of Noah's ﷺ village in return for food. They usually had to give him a whole ox or camel and still he went away complaining. When Noah ﷺ was ordered by Allah to build the Ark he despaired of finding enough wood with which to construct it. Then he was inspired to ask Uj to carry an armload of trees down from the mountains in exchange for a meal. Uj arrived with a mountain of wood, which he dumped at Noah's ﷺ doorstep.

Then he asked for his lunch. Noah ﷺ set before him a normal sized bowl filled with rice and beans. Uj was indignant. Noah ﷺ told him to recite 'Bismillah ar-Rahman ar-Rahim" over the food. Uj would have none of this. His enormous ugly face became as fiery as the anger that fueled him. He hadn't accepted Allah at the time of Adam ﷺ and he had no intention of doing so now. So he shouted at Noah ﷺ "I will never say, Bismillah ar-Rahman ar-Rahim!" And of course in that way he actually said it. Now he ate the food and had never in his life felt so full and satisfied. But still he refused to believe and said it must be some kind of trickery.

So he picked up his mountain of wood and marched angrily back to his mountaintop. However, the scraps and debris that he left behind were sufficient for Noah ﷺ to build his Ark. When the torrential rains began and the water welled up from the ground and the ovens boiled with water, only the creatures that entered into the ark in pairs were saved. But there was one exception. Uj flung himself on the roof of the ark and held on. He held on tightly and some say he helped steer the ark by using his feet as rudders. Noah ﷺ and his family fed him through the chimney of the ark and so, after six months, they arrived together safely on dry land.

At the time of Musa ﷺ Uj was already three or four thousand years old but neither his strength nor his nastiness had diminished. Uj saw what to him looked like tiny men cross over the river. He saw them crawl out of the bushes along the banks in the morning and try to mingle with the people going to market. But they were quite easy to spot because they were so very much smaller than most of the rest of the people. Uj remembered people like that from his childhood. He remembered being tricked by Noah ﷺ. He remembered the one hundred and eighty cold and wet days and nights he had spent draped over the roof of the ark. He remembered the sickening rocking and tossing of the seas and, dreaming of revenge, he ran quickly and scooped up the men of the Banu Israil in one hand.

Uj tucked into the cloth that he wrapped around his waist all twelve of the finest warriors of the Banu Israil and took them to his home. "What should I do with these nasty little bug people?" Uj called out to his wife. "I want to just grind them under my foot, or maybe drown them in my glass of tea, or maybe feed them to my chickens." "Oh no," counseled his wife who was much younger and much smarter. "Their people will wonder where they are and come looking for them. Then we will have to deal with an invasion of the little, annoying creatures. Just set them free and maybe they will return to their people and tell them how strong we are. Most probably none of them will ever come back."

Now Uj listened to his wife. He took the twelve warriors with their little spears and swords and set them down by the river. But first, just to make sure they got the message, Uj reached his arm into the river and pulled out an enormous whale of a fish. He stretched his hand high into the sky and soon the twelve scouts of the Banu Israil could smell the delicious scent of fish kebab. Uj was barbequing his lunch on the surface of the sun.

Yusha ﷺ and Kilab and their companions hurriedly crossed the river and set out in the direction of their camp. Before they had gone too far, but after they had gone far enough to feel safe, the twelve sat down and looked at each other in utter astonishment. Yusha ﷺ was the first to recover and speak. He said that if they returned to their people and told them what they had seen, the people would never obey their prophets or their God. They would never wage war against such an enemy, no matter what divine help was promised. The people were not strong enough yet to face up to such a challenge. So the twelve of them swore an oath not to whisper a word of what they had just seen to any but the two prophets of God.

They returned to the camp of their people. Kilab and Yusha ﷺ kept their oath. They went quickly to the tent of Musa ﷺ and Harun ﷺ and told them what they had seen.

> "They said: O Musa! Lo, a giant people live there." (5:22)

They told no one else but the other ten men did not have as much self-control. They couldn't keep such an astonishing secret to themselves and each of them told only one other person. But that person told another and that one another and so on until the whole camp was rustling with whispers of the disturbing news.

The ten men who had broken their oath were put to death because they were chiefs and they had betrayed their trust and could no longer be relied on. The people, as their leaders had predicted, turned their backs on the promise of their Lord and on the guidance of their prophets. They said to Musa ﷺ and Harun ﷺ, "You may go and fight the giants if you wish but we will not help you. We will sit here in safety and wait for you to come back." Actually they were even more rude and disrespectful than that. They said,

> "So you go with your Lord, and the two of you fight. We will sit here." (5:24)

Musa ﷺ and Harun ﷺ, Yusha ﷺ and Kilab were fed up. They called together the faithful and they turned their backs on the rest of the people. Musa ﷺ raised his hands to his Lord and prayed against his own nation for the first time.

"My Lord! I have control of none but myself and my brother, so distinguish between us and the wrongdoing people." (5:25)

Musa ؑ and Harun ؑ left the encampment of their people and following the direction of the Lord Most High, they determined to face the enemy head-on. They entered the land of Jericho and the first man they came upon was that very Uj ibn Unq. Musa ؑ was 10 cubits tall, and each cubit is the length of a man's forearm from the tip of his fingers to his elbow. Musa's ؑ spear was 10 cubits long and he jumped into the air 10 cubits above the ground. Thirty cubits above the ground Musa ؑ pricked Uj on the anklebone. Uj fell to the ground in pain and some time later he died of that wound. The Prophet Musa ؑ was the one to finally end the very long, and very mean life of Uj ibn Unq.

After this the small army of believers routed the enemy in all their strongholds and fortresses. They did not sneak up on them. They did not plan a subterfuge. They approached the enemy head-on at the gates of their city. Allah gave the victory to His chosen ones regardless of numbers, regardless of strength. Faith and obedience bring victory above all odds.

It is interesting to note that when the Prophet Muhammad ﷺ and the Muslims faced similar odds at the battle of Badr, the Prophet ﷺ gathered his companions around him to ask if they wholeheartedly supported him. It was to be their first military encounter with the enemy, the first battle of a Muslim army. Al-Miqdad ؓ answered the Prophet ﷺ with words he had learned from this story. He said, "We will not answer you as did the people of Musa ؑ: 'Go you and your Lord and fight, we will sit here.' (5:24). But rather we shall fight on your right and on your left and in front of you and behind you." The face of the Prophet ﷺ became bright with happiness and all who were present wished that they had been the one to please him with those words of total commitment. The Muslim army, although greatly outnumbered, went on to rout the enemy.

Meanwhile the Banu Israil were missing their prophets and their chiefs. They were feeling ashamed and sorry for their rebellion. They collected themselves together and decided to try to follow and catch up to the departed army. They set out in the morning in the direction they had seen Musa ﷺ and Harun ﷺ leave. They walked all day, only stopping for a rest in the heat of the day. When the sun set they had not yet found their prophets. They made camp and lay down to sleep.

As the sun rose in the morning they found that they were in exactly the same spot they had set out from the morning before. So they packed up their things, loaded their animals and set out walking again in the direction they determined was right. They walked all day and made camp in the darkness of night. In the morning they awoke to find that they were still in the same place. They knew now that this was not a mistake or a miscalculation. This was the hand of God and they sat down in shame and sorrow to wait and see what would be done with them.

40/48

41.

Bewildered

After several days the Banu Israil saw in the distance what looked like their Prophets and their army approaching. Their hearts lifted. The army was advancing victorious, having accomplished the orders of the Lord and vanquished the tyrants. The land the Lord had promised the Children of Ya'qub was open for them. They were no longer displaced people without a homeland of their own. The Promised Land, the Holy Land, the land of their fathers, Ya'qub ﷺ, Ishaq ﷺ, Ibrahim ﷺ, was theirs once more. Their prophets had returned and would surely free them from the circular trap in which they were caught. They would enter the Holy Land and finally be contented. This was also the hope of Sayyidina Musa ﷺ.

The victorious army entered the encampment, ready to forgive one more time and move on. The people welcomed them and expressed remorse for their disobedience. They had regretted their harsh words and had tried to catch up with the army and join the fighting but try as they might they had only moved in circles. The repentant people told their prophets what had happened when they tried to follow the army. Allah informed His prophet,

"For this land will surely be forbidden to them for forty years and they will wander in the earth, bewildered. So grieve not over the wrongdoing people." (5:26)

As a punishment for again disobeying the direct orders

Allah sent down a pillar of cloud to guide them.

of the Lord, the Banu Israil were sentenced to wander the desert of Tih for forty years until all the disobeying adults had grown old and died. Only their children would be allowed to cross the Jordan River and enter the Promised Land. The prophets shed their feelings of responsibility and sadness over the punishment they had called down on their rebellious people. They accepted the wisdom of the Lord and set about teaching the children. The children would be the ones on whom the new community would be built and they must be well versed in the teachings of the Tawrah.

Allah sent down a pillar of cloud to guide them. Every day the believers packed up their belongings, their tents and their cooking pots. They collected their animals and set out following wherever the cloud would lead them. In circles in the desert of Tih they marched, first the cloud, then the Ark of the Covenant, then the Prophets of God, then the families with all their worldly possessions. When the cloud stopped they stopped. They set down the Ark and set up the Tabernacle around it. They put up their tents and laid out their beds.

When the desert sun beat down upon the people and there was no shade or shelter, the cloud spread itself out over them like a canopy. The Banu Israil walked in the shade of the Lord.

At night the cloud became a pillar of fire. From it they took fire with which to cook and light by which to study. In the morning the cloud returned to lead them on. Every day was like this and every night. In the morning they awoke to find themselves in the place from which they had started. Anyway certainly the rocky landscape looked everywhere the same.

The Banu Israil were going nowhere. The desert of Tih was, and still is, a barren wasteland with only an occasional deep well or dirty pool. The people began to cry out to their prophets that they and their children were thirsty. Musa ﷺ put his stick into the dirty pool and the water flowed out clean and pure. But still they complained because not everyday did the cloud lead them to a pool.

At night the cloud became a pillar of fire.

Allah inspired His Prophet ﷺ to raise his staff and hit a big stone that lay near the camp. The stone became a fountain of water. From each of its four sides flowed three streams of clean drinking water, one for each of the twelve tribes of the Banu Israil. Each morning when they packed up their possessions, their tents, their animals, and the blessed Ark of the Covenant, some say they also placed that rock on a wagon and brought it with them. Wherever the Lord led them, they had their own abundant water supply. But others maintain that since every day they returned to the same spot, the rock stayed where it was until they returned.

After some days or months like this, the lentils, the onions, the wheat, which they had carried out of Egypt, finished. The people began to cry out to their Prophets ﷺ that their children were hungry. The next morning when they awoke they found the dry scrub and bushes around their camp covered with a white flakey substance. In fact the whole desert was covered with this stuff. They tasted it and found it sweet and delicious. They called it manna and it was a gift from God.

Every morning and every night the manna fell like dew upon the dry and barren bushes of the desert of Tih. The people had only to go out and collect it in their aprons or baskets. Always there was just enough to satisfy their hunger, never more. If they tried to put some aside for the next day it melted away without a trace. On Friday, the day before the Sabbath, twice the amount of manna fell and half of that they were able to store for the next day. Because on the seventh day, the Sabbath, no one was allowed to work, even to gather food. All the people rested just as they say that God made the world in six days and on the seventh day He rested. But the Prophet Muhammad ﷺ said that is not true because Allah never gets tired and so never rests.

For many days the people were satisfied and happy with their lot. But eventually they hungered for more familiar and substantial food. The people began to cry to their Prophets ﷺ that their children needed meat. The next morning when they awoke, the Banu Israil found themselves surrounded by little fat birds. They were just lying sleepily on the ground. They did not flap their wings or try to fly away when approached. They lay calmly in the cupped hands of their captor. In fact some say that the birds were already cooked and ready to eat. They called them 'salwa' and they were a gift from God.

The people could only gather as many as they could eat and no more. If they collected more than they needed, the meat went bad. Only on the day before the Sabbath were they able to catch and keep twice as much so that on the Sabbath day they need do no work of any kind.

This situation delighted the people and for many months, or maybe years, they were quite happy. Then they began to notice that their clothes were ripping and getting soiled and ragged. They had no way to weave cloth nor had they access to stores from which to buy it. The people began to cry to their Prophets ﷺ that their children were almost naked. The next morning they awoke to find their clothes repaired, fresh and white and as good as new or better. After this the clothes of the Banu Israil always renewed themselves. In fact the babies were born outfitted with clothes that actually enlarged with them as they grew so that they never needed to be replaced.

Even this perfection did not satisfy forever. Eventually the people began to complain. They were tired of eating the same food every day. It did not matter if it was tasty, healthy, and heavenly. It did not matter if it was satisfying in every way. They were tired of meat and bread made from manna. The people wanted the onions, garlic, and lentils they had enjoyed in the farmlands of Egypt.

"He said: Would you exchange what is higher for what is lower?' (2:61)

Allah told them to leave and return to Egypt if that is what they desired. Presumably some of them did. But most of them repented and stayed in the company of their Prophets ﷺ.

The Banu Israil were not unusually greedy or unappreciative. It is simply the nature of this world that nothing remains pure or unchanged; not love, not pleasure, not satisfaction. Even the very best of it withers, dies, or becomes tasteless. We are not really made for this life; we are made for the next life, the eternal life. In Paradise nothing ever gets old or dies, nothing gets boring or tasteless. It is always reborn and fresh. Contentment and satisfaction, love and companionship, remain ever new and endlessly satisfying.

Not to enter the Promised Land was certainly a punishment for the older generation of Banu Israil. But the wandering in the desert was not a punishment for the innocent youth. It was a training. It was as if they were in seclusion, away from the influences of the unbelieving world that surrounded them. The fact that its duration was forty years, like forty days, is further indication of this. They had only each other and their Prophets ﷺ to guide them. Musa ﷺ and Harun ﷺ and their twelve thousand righteous companions taught the others by example and by strong words. They taught the children the Tawrah, both the written and the unwritten. Prayer, sacrifice, and charity became a fact of everyday life and as accepted as breathing.

During these forty years of training, Allah supplied His chosen ones with all the necessities. They had food, drink and clothing of the most basic and perfect kind. They had no excess, no reason for greed or envy or competition. They had no need to ask from anyone anything. They had only to follow the cloud, collect their dinner and soak up the wisdom and love that Allah Almighty showered upon them. It was a life without luxury but a life of simplicity and devotion. They had no activity other than the worship of their Creator. They had no purpose other than that.

The Sign Of The Fish

The Banu Israil were condemned to wander the desert of Tih but the Prophets ﷺ and the twelve thousand righteous were not. At some point when Sayyidina Musa ﷺ was teaching his people, they were so astonished by his wisdom and knowledge that they asked him if there was anyone else in the whole world who knew as much as he. Musa ﷺ thought for a while and in all humility he answered that he thought that probably there was not.

But Allah Almighty heard his words and was not pleased. Nobody can know or even guess the extent of Allah's creations. He is "Lord of the worlds". How many worlds? How many creatures? To whom He gives knowledge and of what kind and to what extent is in itself unknowable. So Allah informed His servant Musa ﷺ, in order to teach him, of the existence of another of His servants who had knowledge of things of which Musa ﷺ was ignorant.

Musa ﷺ was neither hurt nor humiliated to be chided by his Lord. He had not been speaking from pride when he had stated that he thought he was the most knowledgeable of Allah's servants. He was being truthful to the extent of his understanding. Now he was filled with a great longing to meet this man of knowledge and to learn from him. Because the sincere search for useful knowledge has been made incumbent on all men.

Allah informed Musa ﷺ that he could meet this man at the place where the "two seas (or rivers) meet" (18:60). He was instructed to take food with him and when that food disappeared

"They forgot their fish and it took its way into the water by a marvel." (18:63)

he would find the man he sought. Musa ﷺ slipped away from his people. He took with him his young companion Yusha ﷺ who had proven himself to be so trustworthy and dependable and who would eventually be made the prophet to follow him. They packed a basket of provisions for their journey. Allah told them to take with them a dry, salted fish because that fish would be a sign for them.

They began walking, some think in the Nile delta, or Alexandria. Some think near the Red Sea. Some even say in Iraq or in Turkey. Allah has not informed us of its actual, physical location. They walked for some time. One evening they stopped to rest near a big rock close to the water. Musa ﷺ lay down to sleep while Yusha ﷺ stood guard. When he awoke the pair continued their journey. Tired, they stopped for breakfast. Musa ﷺ reached into the basket and found the fish was gone. Just then Yusha ﷺ remembered what had happened.

Allah says many times in The Quran that mankind was made forgetful. This is why he needs to be constantly reminded and why remembrance (dhikr) is required of him. But in spite of all the signs the gracious Lord sends us still we forget. When they had stopped by the rock to rest Yusha ﷺ had seen the dry, salted fish wriggle out of the basket and jump into the water. Then, mysteriously, the water stopped its flow and opened a tunnel through which the now alive fish made its way, just as Allah opened a way for the Banu Israil through the sea.

Yusha ﷺ could not believe that he had forgotten to mention this to his master. "Only the devil made me forget," (18:63) he said. The two turned around and retraced their steps. The sign Musa ﷺ was waiting for was at the rock. When they reached the rock they saw a man covered in a cloak sitting on the ground. They approached him and he knew Musa ﷺ immediately and that he was sent as a Messenger to the Banu Israil. But he was not particularly anxious to take Musa ﷺ on as his disciple.

This man is identified in The Quran only as "a servant from among Our servants." (18:65). The Prophet Muhammad

ﷺ, however, identified him as the immortal saint known as "Al-Khidr" ؑ, the Green Man. Some scholars say that he was an ordinary soldier in the army of Alexander the Great, who was sent to fetch water for the troops when they were somewhere in Asia. He happened upon a lake, called The Water of Life, and fell in. From this he gained immortality. But he must have been extraordinary from the outset because long life does not guarantee wisdom nor does Allah's favor fall on the undeserving.

It is said that if you are lucky enough to meet him you might see his coat blow open and catch a flash of shimmering green. Or you might notice a green glow that surrounds him. Where he walks the grass and trees grow green. Even if he walks in the desert or in the snow, a trail of green follows him. The Prophet ﷺ said "Al-Khidr was called so because he sat upon a white wasteland that became green after his sitting on it." Allah gave him the ability to bring to life anything he touches. That is why the resurrection of the fish was a sign of his presence.

Al-Khidr ؑ is considered by some to be a prophet. He will continue to live until the end of time. He has been the teacher of prophets and of saints and continues to keep company with the friends of God. He wanders the earth in the service of his Lord.

Once when the Prophet ﷺ was traveling with his companion, Anas Ibn Malik ؓ, they heard a noise in the distance. The Prophet ﷺ sent Anas ؓ to see what it was. He found a man crying and praying, asking God to accept him as a member of the community of Muhammad ﷺ. Anas ؓ asked his name and he replied that he was Al-Khidr ؑ. He sent greetings to the Prophet ﷺ who in turn sent salams and then prayed to God to accept Al-Khidr's ؑ plea.

The companions of the Prophet Muhammad ﷺ also related that at the time of the Prophet's ﷺ death they heard a voice coming from a dark corner of the room in which he was lying. It was a small room and crowded with mourners but they clearly heard condolences being given in a distinctly unfamiliar voice. Although most did not see from whom the voice was coming, the ones who knew said it came from Al-Khidr ﷺ.

Musa ﷺ asked Al-Khidr ﷺ to let him be his companion and learn from him the special knowledge he had been given by God. But Al-Khidr ﷺ was not very positive about the possibility of this. He said:

"You cannot bear with me. How can you bear with what you do not encompass in knowledge?" (18:67-68)

In other words, if Allah has not prepared you for this knowledge I cannot give it to you. If you do not have the ability to understand how can I teach you? But Musa ﷺ pleaded with Al-Khidr ﷺ, promising to be patient and open-minded. At last Al-Khidr ﷺ offered to let him accompany him, on the condition that he not question him about anything he might see. Musa ﷺ promised. They sent Yusha ﷺ back to his people while Musa ﷺ and Al-Khidr ﷺ went on together.

$$\frac{42}{48}$$

43.

The Beak Of The Bird

Musa ﷺ and Al-Khidr ﷺ journeyed together for a while until they came to a great river or sea. They looked for a boat that would ferry them to the other side. The captain of one boat recognized something special in the two men and offered to transport them free of charge. They boarded the boat and it set sail.

As they sat on the deck watching the shore recede into the distance a small bird landed on the bow beside them. It dipped its head to drink from the water and a tiny drop could be seen still hanging from the end of its beak. Al-Khidr ﷺ turned to his companion and commented that that tiny drop was to the wide river as the combined knowledge of both Musa ﷺ and Al-Khidr ﷺ were to the oceans of Divine Knowledge. The knowledge of these two chosen men of God was not even a significant drop of what there was to know.

Halfway across the river Al-Khidr ﷺ took out a blade and, without attracting attention, made a hole in the bottom of the boat until the water began to ooze in. Musa ﷺ was shocked. The sailors had been kind and generous enough to take them without cost across the river and Al-Khidr ﷺ was jeopardizing their lives and vandalizing their property.

Musa ﷺ was a prophet of God. He was a lawgiver and a leader of men. He was accustomed to judging and discriminating. How could he remain silent? He instinctively and sincerely questioned the outrageous behavior he had witnessed in his teacher. Al-Khidr ﷺ responded by reminding Musa ﷺ of his promise not to question anything he saw. Musa ﷺ, still confused,

A drop from the oceans of Divine Knowledge.

but not wanting to fail, promised not to forget again, but to hold his tongue and refrain from judgment.

Once on the far side they followed the river until they entered a town. Along the road they saw a group of small boys playing ball. Al-Khidr ﷺ grabbed the most handsome of the group, laid him down on the ground and slaughtered him. Now Musa ﷺ had been reminded and he had not forgotten, but this action could not be right. He could not let such a crime go without protest. Again Al-Khidr ﷺ reprimanded him and reminded him of his promise.

Again Musa ﷺ apologized and promised that he would not voice his doubts a third time. Al-Khidr ﷺ was certain that Musa ﷺ would not be able to keep his promise and perhaps Musa ﷺ also had his doubts. Musa ﷺ promised that if he failed one more time Al-Khidr ﷺ could part company with him. And it was this promise for which, thousands of years later, the Prophet Muhammad ﷺ was sorry. For if Musa ﷺ had not made this secondary promise he might have lasted longer in the company of Al-Khidr ﷺ and all of us might have learned a little more of his special knowledge. However, Musa ﷺ promised that if he failed a third time he would leave Al-Khidr ﷺ to travel on alone.

They left the town in haste

and walked at a fast pace until nightfall. They were tired and hungry when a small village came into sight. They stood in the public square as the sun set and asked where travelers could find food or shelter but no one showed the slightest interest in offering strangers any form of hospitality. Eventually they found a ruined building outside of town in which, hungry and thirsty, they settled down for the night.

In the morning they noticed that the wall they had sheltered against was leaning heavily and about to fall. Al-Khidr ﷺ spent all the next day repairing this wall and shoring up the old house. By evening Musa ﷺ was completely exasperated. They had spent a full day fixing the property of people who had not even had the decency to give two weary travelers a bite of food. Musa ﷺ felt that if they needed to repair the wall, they should have at least asked for compensation and received a hot meal.

The Prophet Muhammad ﷺ said that the first time Musa ﷺ violated his promise was because he forgot. The second time he made a secondary condition to his promise. The third time he both intentionally and knowingly broke his promise. He was not able, or perhaps willing, to keep company with Al-Khidr ﷺ. And now Al-Khidr ﷺ declared that the time had come for them to go their separate ways. Musa ﷺ had promised so he had no recourse.

Before they separated Al-Khidr ﷺ offered to explain the wisdom of the actions Musa ﷺ had found so difficult to accept. First he explained:

"I did not do it of my own accord." (18:82)

Meaning that what he did he was instructed by Allah to do. He was an obedient servant to an All-Knowing Master.

The boat on which they had sailed belonged to righteous, God-fearing men. There was a tyrant down river who was gathering together an army to wage war on a neighboring kingdom. He was confiscating all the boats in the area to serve as his transport. The soldiers would not be interested in a leaking boat. By damaging the boat Al-Khidr ﷺ had actually saved it from being confiscated.

Al-Khidr ﷺ had killed the little boy not out of anger but because he was destined to be immoral and wicked. His parents were believers and upright. They might, out of love, have followed their son into disbelief. He took the life of the child while he was still innocent so that he and his parents were spared both sin and its punishment. In place of the boy Allah later gave the parents a daughter who was to become the ancestor of seventy prophets.

As for the wall, it belonged to two orphans whose names were Asram and Sarim. Under the wall their righteous father had hidden a treasure. If the wall fell their greedy, unscrupulous neighbors would have stolen their property. By repairing the wall Al-Khidr ﷺ had kept the inheritance of the orphans secure until they could grow up and claim it for themselves. There is a Hadith in which the Prophet ﷺ said, "God protects the pious man, his sons and grandsons, as well as the spot on which he dwells and its neighborhood, and he remains in God's protection and shelter."

Not one of his actions was done of his own volition. Al-Khidr ﷺ is a perfect servant of Allah following the special knowledge given to him. Musa ﷺ also was a perfect servant of Allah following the knowledge given to him. Some say one represents the outer knowledge, the laws of this world, and the other represents the inner wisdom, the secrets behind the events of this world. But perhaps it would be better and more accurate to say they represent only two levels out of the limitless levels of God's knowledge

What is interesting is that although Musa ﷺ objected strongly to the actions of Al-Khidr ﷺ and seemed to be unable to remain patient with them, all three events have close parallels in Musa's ﷺ own life. Just as Al-Khidr ﷺ jeopardized the boat in order to preserve it, so Ummi Musa ﷺ placed her baby into the ark and set it adrift on the river in order to save him. Just as Al

Khidr ﷺ killed a boy who was to be a tyrant so Musa ﷺ killed an oppressor of his people. Just as Al-Khidr ﷺ repaired the falling wall for the service of Allah and not for payment, so Musa ﷺ helped the daughters of Shuayb ﷺ at the well, seeking reward only from his Lord.

With these obvious parallels it must be that Musa ﷺ understood to some degree what was happening. He was neither ignorant nor impatient. It simply was not his position or role on this earth to act outside of the law. But perhaps, just as Yusha ﷺ had forgotten to mention the resurrection of the dried fish so in this case Musa ﷺ was made to forget his own history. Knowledge is clearly a grant from Allah Almighty. What is meant for us we understand. What is not meant for us we cannot grasp, no matter how hard we may want to.

As Al-Khidr ﷺ finished explaining, a small deer stepped out of the bushes and lay down in front of them. Al-Khidr ﷺ stretched out his hand and the little deer lay dead. Musa ﷺ was astonished to see that not only had the deer died but also that half of it was skinned and roasted, ready to eat. Al-Khidr ﷺ accepted his dinner without surprise or comment. He instructed Musa ﷺ to skin and cook the raw half for himself.

Musa ﷺ began to obey but hunger and the smell of the roasted meat overwhelmed him. He asked Al-Khidr ﷺ to share his cooked half with him. But every time Musa ﷺ picked up a delicious piece of meat and brought it to his mouth it turned raw and bloody. There was nothing to do but skin the other half, cook and then eat. Al-Khidr ﷺ explained that since Musa ﷺ expected payment for his work on repairing the wall, he likewise would have to work for his dinner. Al-Khidr ﷺ on the other hand had done what he did with no expectation other than serving God. For this God served him by providing him with food already prepared. He did not have to lift a hand in providing for himself.

After they had finished dinner Al-Khidr ﷺ picked up the hide of the deer and blew on it. It immediately came to life and the little deer bounded into the bushes. Musa ﷺ carried in his hand the Law, the Shariat of Allah that follows the rules of consequences, cause and effect. Al-Khidr ﷺ carried in his hand, however, the Qudrat of Allah, the Power of Allah that can simply say – "Be" and it is. After this Musa ﷺ and Al-Khidr ﷺ bade each other farewell and each went on his way following the path the Lord had assigned to him. Musa ﷺ returned to his people, the Banu Israil, and brought them a deeper and a wider understanding of the world and its Creator.

The search for knowledge has been made an obligation for us. The Prophet ﷺ said, "Seek knowledge even if it is in China." In fact it is said that the Prophet Yusha ﷺ at some point in his life did travel all the way to China to learn their wisdom and to share with them his knowledge of Allah, the One God, and His commandments.

$$\frac{43}{48}$$

44.

The Tail Of The Cow

The Quran mentions an incident that took place at some point during the time the Banu Israil were wandering in the wilderness. There was a wealthy man of the Banu Israil named 'Ameel, who had no children. He decided to take two of his nephews into his care and eventually make them his heirs. But these boys were ungrateful and envious. After some years they got sick of taking care of their uncle and pretending they loved him. They got tired of waiting for him to die and his fortune to become theirs. They took matters into their own hands and murdered their uncle. Then they took his body and laid it on the border between the camps of their tribe and that of one of the other tribes of Israil.

In the morning they pretended to find his body. They wailed and they cried so that everyone came running. No one could imagine who would have done such a terrible deed. The old man was very generous and loved by all. It must have been some jealous member of the other tribe who had killed him and left his body on the border.

But all the members of the other tribe protested ardently that they had not done such a ghastly thing. Each and everyone was questioned and a reason or a motive could not be found. They went to Musa ﷺ and asked him to judge between them or tell them what they should do. Musa ﷺ consulted his Lord. Allah Almighty revealed,

"And indeed Allah commands you to slaughter a cow." (2:67)

"Ask your Lord what kind of cow she is?" (2:70)

Instead of accepting the word of their Prophet ﷺ the people first questioned whether Musa ﷺ was telling the truth. Then they began to stall because they didn't understand or because they didn't want to sacrifice a precious cow. So they asked, what kind of a cow? Allah answered them,

"She is a cow neither too old nor too young but in between. So do as you are commanded" (2:68)

But they did not do as they were commanded. Rather they asked, what color should the cow be? Again the Almighty responded to their delaying tactics by giving more details:

"She is a yellow cow, bright in color, pleasing to the beholders." (2: 69)

Allah Almighty says that yellow is pleasing to the eye and seeing something beautiful and pleasing will make us happy. Because of this Ali ibn Abi Talib ؓ recommended the wearing of yellow shoes to bring happiness and reduce sorrow. But this did not satisfy the Banu Israil. Be more specific they asked. All cows look the same to us. Now they were given a description truly hard to satisfy.

"She is a cow neither broken-in to till the soil nor to water the fields, sound, and with no blemish on her." (2: 71

If they had accepted the first answer, any cow would have probably been acceptable. But because they doubted and argued and questioned, each time the cow became more and more specific. Finally they had to find a very rare and particular animal, not an easy task at all. At the time of the last Prophet, Muhammad ﷺ, God warned the Muslims,

"Do you intend to question your Messenger as Musa was questioned previously?" (2: 108)

Muhammad ﷺ warned his people that one of the worst sins was to ask unnecessary questions that might result in something permitted becoming forbidden. Some things you do not need to know. Once you know them you become responsible for your knowledge and, rather than clarifying things, it can make things much more difficult.

The Banu Israil were charged with the task of finding this most particular cow. As always, every little act of the Almighty has wisdom behind it. Even evil does the work of the Creator.

Among another tribe there was a family. The father had been a poor but righteous man. When he sensed that the time of his death was drawing near he raised his hands to Allah and welcomed death but entrusted the welfare of his young son and wife to the care of Allah Almighty. Allah inspired the man to take the calf he had tied up behind his tent and let it loose into the wilderness. The man informed his wife that Allah would provide for them. If ever they were in desperate straights she must send the son into the wilderness to find the calf.

The boy grew up and was an obedient and pious boy. He took care of his mother and did what she advised him. He gathered wood and sold it to the people to fuel their fires. This was sufficient for his and his mother's daily needs but it was not enough for him to marry or begin a life of his own. His mother told him one day that the time had come for him to go out into the wilderness and call the calf of his father.

The boy did not know what to expect. It had been a while since his father had died. How was he supposed to find this cow, if it was still living, or even know it was the right one? But he obeyed the wishes of his mother. He went into the scrubby hills behind their tent and called loudly into the emptiness for the calf.

To his great amazement he soon heard a lowing sound and over the distant hill he saw a beautiful, warm yellow cow come loping along, her tail swinging behind her. She came right up to him as if she recognized him and licked his face and hands.

He put a rope around her neck and brought her to his mother.

His mother told him he should take the cow to market the next morning and sell her for the best price he could get. He followed his mother's advice and the next morning he took the cow to market to sell her. On the way he met a man who offered to buy his cow for double the price that the boy had considered asking. This confused the boy very much and he said that first he would have to consult his mother.

He went home. His mother was delighted and told him to return the next day and to accept the price because it was very generous. The boy left for the market early the next morning. On the way he met another man and this man offered three times the price for the cow. Again the boy was confused. Because this was not exactly what his mother had instructed him he returned home.

His mother was a little frustrated that her son had not sold the cow but when she heard the reason she was overjoyed. She carefully instructed him to return to market next morning and to accept whatever price they offered him for the cow.

Next morning he set out and on the road he met a man, who, although he looked like an ordinary person, was actually an angel. This angel was sent by Allah to keep the trust of the father, to watch over the boy and take care of him. Now he instructed the boy not to sell the cow for anything less than its weight in gold. The boy went on to the market, where all the men began to fight with each other to buy his cow. He refused to sell for any price less than its full weight in gold. Finally they agreed to put all their money together and to give him what he asked.

What a high price the Banu Israil had to pay for their idle curiosity and their cow! And what a wise man he was to leave his family in the exclusive care of the Almighty.

Now the believers were ordered to sacrifice the cow and strike the murdered man with the tail. When they did this the dead man sat up and pointed out his two nephews as his murderers.

"And when you killed a man and disagreed concerning it and Allah revealed what you were hiding. And We said, Smite him with some of it. Thus Allah brings the dead to life and shows you His signs so that you may understand." (2:72-73)

In this way the truth was made known and justice was done. It became clear that even evil does the bidding of Allah: even evil must be a servant of Goodness, and within all things there is a hidden wisdom.

משה

44/48

45.

Attributes Of The Prophets

There are two attributes of Allah Almighty of which all the prophets partake: Majesty (al-Jalal) and Beauty (al-Jamal). All of the prophets exhibit these two qualities in different combinations. It is said that the Prophet Muhammad ﷺ was a perfect balance of the two. The Prophet Ibrahim ﷺ was also an equal combination, which is perhaps why the Prophet Muhammad ﷺ said that of all the prophets he was most similar to Ibrahim ﷺ. The Prophet Isa ﷺ exhibited mostly Beauty, as did the Prophet Yusuf ﷺ and the Prophet Harun ﷺ. The Prophet Musa ﷺ on the other hand exhibited predominantly the Divine attribute of Majesty. When he spoke even the Divine Throne trembled.

In appearance the Prophet Musa ﷺ had brown skin and was very tall and strong. The Prophet Muhammad ﷺ was riding one day with his companions in the valley of Azraq. He said, "As for Musa ﷺ, he is a large, brown man on a red camel whose reins are made of palm fiber. It is as if I am looking at him while he is going into the valley, calling the talbiyah (the supplication made on Hajj – Here I am O Lord, at Your service)."

Musa ﷺ was a shepherd by training and by nature. A shepherd does not walk in front of his sheep expecting them to follow nicely behind him. A shepherd walks behind his sheep, using his staff to keep them together, running, prodding, rounding up the stragglers and the rebellious. He will even carry the weak and encourage the old. If there is anything in his power he will do it in order to bring each and every one of those under his charge to safety. Musa ﷺ would even stand up to the Lord

The Beautiful - Al Jamal. The Majestic - Al-Jalal

Almighty to plead for the forgiveness of his people. At one point he argued,

"My Lord. If you had willed, You could have destroyed them previously, and me as well. Would You destroy us for what the foolish among us have done?" (7:155)

It is often said that the Prophet Musa ﷺ was angry and impatient. He killed a man when he was young. As a prophet he smashed to the ground the holy tablets on which the Lord had written the Tawrah. The Jews even say that he was denied entry into the Holy Land because of his anger: he struck the boulder several times with his stick instead of commanding it with words to produce water for the people. But in the Hadith Musa ﷺ is portrayed as the embodiment of patience and forbearance. His Lord tested him severely, first by means of the Pharaoh who would not listen and then by means of his people, the Banu Israil, who kept doubting him and disobeying. In fact the Hadith of Ibn Abbas ﷺ that recounts the story of Musa ﷺ as told by the Prophet Muhammad ﷺ are collectively called Al Futun, The Trials. Musa ﷺ was often tried and remained patient.

He was patient but unyielding. For forty years he stayed by Pharaoh's side, at first reminding, then warning, finally threatening. For another forty years he led the Banu Israil through hardship and betrayal until they were purged and purified and fit to be God's chosen. He did this on orders from Allah, not according to his own whims. Once he received Divine Orders he followed them, never turning away or doubting. His actions did not originate with him so it is fair to assume that his reactions also did not reflect his own will but rather that of his Divine Master.

Anger has been defined as the absence of mercy. But since Anger is also an Attribute of God and since God is Merciful above all else, Divine Anger must in some way also be a mercy. The purpose of human anger is to destroy opposition and gain power. The purpose of Divine Anger is to shatter evil in order to protect everyone. A child, who tries to rush into the street after a ball and is prevented by his mother, has eyes only for his own desire and experiences his mother's loving restraint as cruelty. Perhaps the occasions in which Musa ﷺ appeared to be angry can best be understood in this way.

He tried to prevent the slave driver from acting unjustly but it resulted in a struggle to the death. He tried to offer Pharaoh sound advice and mercy but all his actions were continually perceived as a threat. He brought the Word of God down from the mountain of Sinai and found his people in the act of sinning, unable and unworthy to receive it. He smashed the great tablets to the ground thus also shattering the evil. In no instance did he use his anger for a selfish aim or simply to vent his own frustration. His great power and majesty allowed him to use anger as a tool to achieve the most merciful ends. But as Sayyidina Muhammad ﷺ noted, if Musa ﷺ had waited only a bit longer before using this most powerful and decisive of tools, we may all have learned so much more.

In Arabic Musa ﷺ has two titles derived from The Quran. One is "Kalimullah": he who converses with God. Allah spoke to him and he spoke back. He became the spokesman for Allah's Word. The other is "Najiullah", the confidant of Allah. He spoke to God as God spoke to him. He held nothing back either out of reverence or out of fear. If he did not understand he said so. If he did not agree he said so. No other prophet that we know of could speak with this kind of familiarity to his Lord. Because it was his nature and devoid of false pride or self-serving anger; because it was genuine and his right, Allah allowed it and answered him in the same direct way.

"And mention in the Book, Musa. Truly he was a chosen one and a messenger, a prophet." (19:51)

The word, translated here as chosen, is 'mukhlas', a derivative of the word 'ikhlas' meaning sincere. But a mukhlas is one who is made sincere, purified of anything insincere or counter to his real being. This kind of sincerity is God-given. It is not a state that man can achieve by striving but rather a state that God chooses for him. In the sight of his Lord he is utterly and thoroughly genuine. This is Allah's description of His servant Musa ﷺ.

Harun ﷺ, on the other hand, was more gentle and reserved, beautiful and forbearing. Allah says in His Quran,

"And We bestowed on him (Musa) of Our Mercy his brother Harun, a prophet." (19:53).

This means that not only was Harun ﷺ given to his brother Musa ﷺ in a gesture of mercy by the Lord Most High but also that Harun ﷺ originated out of the Divine Attribute of Mercy; he was formed from it.

The Prophet Muhammad ﷺ saw him on the Night Journey in the fifth heaven and described his great beauty. He had inherited this from his grandfather, Sayyidina Yusuf ﷺ, who was said to have possessed half of all the beauty Allah created for this whole world. The Prophet ﷺ compared Harun ﷺ to Sayyidina Ali ﷺ. Once when the Prophet ﷺ left Ali ﷺ to stay in Madina to watch over the family while he took the other men on an expedition, Ali ﷺ expressed dismay. The Prophet ﷺ told him: "Are you not content O Ali, that you should be unto me as Harun was unto Musa, except that after me there will be no other prophet?"

Harun ﷺ was chosen to be the first High Priest of Israil. He was the only one permitted to enter the Holy of Holies, the resting place of the Tabut. If anyone else entered they would be destroyed, consumed by fire. The other tribes contested this position and Allah confirmed His choice of Harun ﷺ by making his staff flower. Perhaps this was a symbol of the fact that, to this day, the priests must be chosen from the descendants of Harun ﷺ. The descendants of Musa ﷺ, however, do not seem to have been distinguished from others.

If Musa ﷺ represents Truth and Righteousness, then Harun ﷺ represents Mercy and Forbearance. And it is not surprising that most of the Banu Israil preferred the second although they obeyed and respected the first. So Harun ﷺ led the Banu Israil in crossing the sea. They followed him trustingly into the strange and fearful canyons between the walls of water. Musa ﷺ on the other hand waited to be the last to cross. He waited until all of his flock was safely on the path. He herded them before him, goading the reluctant and encouraging the slow.

People do not always appreciate being goaded, prodded and pushed. They seemed to have loved Harun ﷺ more than they did Musa ﷺ. But they did not obey him to the same degree. They threatened to kill him when he remonstrated with them about the golden calf. They accused Musa ﷺ of being jealous of their love for his brother. Yet it was by Musa's ﷺ request that Harun ﷺ had been granted prophethood in the first place and there can be no more generous or sharing act than this.

It is clear that these two brothers worked together in harmony, the one balancing the other. It was Musa ﷺ who had the fearlessness and strength to speak directly to the Lord, and it was Harun ﷺ who had the eloquence and gentleness to communicate the message to the people.

משה

$$\frac{45}{48}$$

46.

A Marvelous Tree

One day Allah spoke to Musa ﷺ and requested that he bring his brother Harun ﷺ to a meeting at the top of a certain mountain. Some say this was in the thirtieth year of the wandering, some say it was in the early days of the fortieth year. Still others assert it was in the thirty-third year of wandering in circles in the wilderness. His appointment was with the Angel of Death, Azrail ﷺ, and it could not be missed nor put off.

Musa ﷺ asked his brother to accompany him to the distant mountain, which is situated in today's Jordan and bears the name of Jabal Harun. Harun ﷺ was getting old. He was over one hundred years and he tired more quickly than he used to. It was a long hard climb to the top. He leaned heavily on his staff and stopped to rest many times. Finally they reached a spot on the mountain from which they could view the panorama of craggy mountains and winding valleys of the now so familiar wilderness stretched out before them.

At this spot they found a tree of such remarkable and unusual beauty that neither of the Prophets ﷺ had ever seen its like. There was a small house under the tree and a garden in which a bed was laid, covered with thick carpets and backed with soft pillows. Sayyidina Harun ﷺ was tired and sleepy and the bed looked so inviting that he felt irresistibly drawn to lay himself down on its comfortable cushions. However, he felt shy to do so because the owner was not at home and so he could not ask for permission.

Musa ﷺ encouraged his brother to lie down and rest.

Neither of the prophets had seen the like of that marvelous tree.

He offered to sit nearby and keep watch. If the owner came home he would speak and make apologies for him. But Harun ﷺ was uncomfortable with that also. He didn't want to make his brother sit up the whole time and he also did not want to be the only one who was to blame. He asked Musa ﷺ to lie down with him, and the two of them would rest in the shade of that marvelous tree.

Musa ﷺ agreed and they both stretched themselves out on the wide and comfortable pillows. As soon as Harun ﷺ lay down, Azrail ﷺ, the Angel of Death, appeared before him and gently invited him to the meeting with his Lord. Harun ﷺ voiced his dismay with Musa ﷺ for he had hidden the true purpose of their journey and had given no warning. But he knew in his heart that this meeting was inevitable and he was accepting, ready to obey. Harun ﷺ bade his brother farewell and turned to the Angel of God and willingly gave him his last breath.

Musa ﷺ did the funeral prayers for his beloved brother and spent the afternoon in mourning for his trusted companion of almost eighty years. As the sun sank lower in the sky he began to worry about what the people would say when he returned to them without Harun ﷺ. He knew his people and he knew they would suspect all kinds of things. He took a good look around to make sure he knew the place so that he could bring the Banu Israil to the blessed spot, the final resting place of their beloved Prophet ﷺ.

As Musa ﷺ prepared to bury his brother, Allah had angels lift the bed from the ground and raise it into the sky with the body of Harun ﷺ lying gently upon it. Musa ﷺ returned to his people and as he suspected they immediately began to question him suspiciously about the whereabouts of Harun ﷺ.

Harun ﷺ had lived his whole life among them. He had suffered through the tyranny and slavery of Pharaoh. He had endured all the hardships by their side. He had counseled them and supported them through all the difficult years. His family had suffered as they had suffered. He had always guided them with a gentle hand. He had been the one to lead the way for

Photo Martin Gray/National Geographic Stock.

The Maqam of the Prophet Harun ﷺ on top of Jabal Harun in Jordan overlooking the ancient city of Petra.

them across the sea, to be the first to set foot on the dry path between the walls of water. He had, by his example, shown them the way through danger and difficulty. Even with the incident of the golden calf he had counseled them correctly but had not punished them or threatened them. He was soft hearted and reasonable.

Musa ﷺ on the other hand, had been almost a foreigner. He had been raised in the house of the enemy. While they slaved in the fields of the Pharaoh, he was resting in the palace. Although he had given up everything to take their side, still he had, in doing so, committed a violent act and had to flee the country. For many years he had been in exile and had not shared in the agony of his people. When he returned with the Word of God it seemed that he only increased their pain and suffering. He was fierce in his support of the Lord and sometimes it seemed like anger. His justice was unbending. His devotion to his mission was uncompromising. The veil that he wore to hide the divine light that radiated from his blessed face also separated him from the common men. All of these things made Musa ﷺ appear distant, unapproachable and a bit frightening.

Now he had returned from an innocuous walk, without his brother. What had happened? Why had they not seen or heard anything? Maybe there was something to hide. Whatever it was, they felt that their loss was great, terrible, and sudden and they were unprepared. They wanted to blame someone. So Musa ﷺ took a group of the elders with him up the mountain to the spot where Harun ﷺ had breathed his last. The beautiful tree was gone. The house, the garden, the bed, the body of his brother, they were all gone.

Now the people began to suspect all kinds of things. They actually accused Musa ﷺ, their fierce, upright, prophet, the one who was chosen by Allah Almighty to be His friend and to whom He spoke intimately on a regular basis, they accused Musa ﷺ of murdering his brother. The people muttered that Musa ﷺ had been jealous of the love the people felt for his brother, Harun ﷺ, and so he had decided to get rid of him. Musa ﷺ, although he was expecting some reaction, was still astonished at the degree to which their accusations went. He said:

"O my people, why do you injure me, while you certainly know that I am God's messenger to you?" (61:5)

Musa ﷺ fell on his knees and made prostration to his Lord asking for His aid in countering the false accusations of his own people. At that moment Allah had the angels bring the bed with the body of Harun ﷺ still upon it, back down from the heavens into clear view of the people. Harun ﷺ was made to breathe again and he sat up on his bed and spoke. He said that his brother had not harmed him and that he had consented willingly to go with the Angel of Death to the long awaited meeting with his Lord. For the last time he acted as his brother's advocate, speaking eloquently in Musa's ﷺ defense, as he had been entrusted to do, so long ago by the Lord.

After this, Harun ﷺ lay back down and he and the bed ascended into the heavens and were never seen again. A mosque was built on the spot where the tree had stood and where the Prophet Harun ﷺ had breathed his last. And from the descendants of Harun ﷺ have come a long line of holy men and women, saints and teachers, priests and prophets: a marvelous family tree.

    May Allah bless Sayyidina Harun ﷺ whose example of sanctity and gentleness, obedience and humility, continue to inspire us and revive our hope.

46/48

47.

An Angel's Eye

It is related that Sayyidina Musa ﷺ at some time in his life suffered from a prolonged illness. He spent many days and weeks lying on a mat on the ground. The people came to visit him, worried for his health, and each of them gave him advice. One suggested this herb, another swore by that remedy. He listened to them all but refused to take anything they offered or do anything they recommended. He said that he was content to wait for Allah, the Creator of sickness and health, to heal and relieve him.

But his ill health continued in spite of his prayers and his patience. Finally Allah spoke directly to His servant Musa ﷺ and asked him why he did not take the medicine the people had offered. Was He, Allah the Creator of sickness and health, not also the Creator of the herbs and remedies? Then Musa ﷺ took the medicines given him and recovered quickly.

But Musa ﷺ remembered this period of ill health and he always petitioned his Lord not to try him again with sickness. Allah promised Musa ﷺ good health for the rest of his life. In fact, it is said that Allah Almighty took a shirt from the divine treasuries. This shirt was imbued with health and wellbeing and Allah gave it to Musa ﷺ to wear until his dying day.

But Sayyidina Musa ﷺ did not like the idea of dying either. He asked his Lord if there was not some way other than death. But Allah was firm with His prophet. All living creatures must taste of death. Finally the Lord promised His friend that he would never take his soul without first asking his permission. Musa ﷺ continued to petition his Lord because he knew that

"so that you [Musa] might be raised under My eye." (20:39)

The Maqam of the Prophet Musa ﷺ in Israel just outside of Jericho.

he might be tricked into giving permission. Allah promised His servant that he would never send him death until he had dug his own grave. This way for sure Musa ﷺ thought he would have had to be consenting.

The days passed in the wilderness until forty years had elapsed. Musa ﷺ was one hundred and twenty years old. He had been forty when the Lord spoke to him from the burning bush. He had spent forty years in Egypt struggling with Pharaoh. He had spent another forty years teaching his people the Tawrah in the wilderness. Musa ﷺ was hoping to be the one to lead his people into the Promised Land, the land of their ancestors. All the men who had refused to follow the prophets in their fight against the giants, had died in the wilderness. All of Musa's ﷺ contemporaries and friends, except for Yusha ﷺ and Kilab ؓ had been buried in the desert of Tih. The young generation was strong and faithful. There was new life ahead for Israil.

There is the possibility that Musa ﷺ died on the mountain of Tur forty years earlier and that he was resurrected at that time. If this is correct then he was taken alive into the heavens to await the Judgment Day. There exist, however, accounts of his death and burial at the end of the forty years in the desert and only

Allah knows the truth.

One morning as Musa ﷺ was sitting in the shade beside his tent a visitor suddenly appeared. Musa ﷺ recognized him at once as the angel Azrail ﷺ, the Angel of Death. At that time it is said that the angel came openly and visibly to everyone whose soul he was sent to take. Azrail ﷺ had a fearsome appearance. His eyes were cold and hard; they had seen many pleading faces and many tears. His lips were firmly set; it had been eons since they had parted in a smile. His hands were like iron; they had torn many a mother from a weeping child and many a child from a pleading parent.

Musa ﷺ was not pleased to see this servant of Allah. As the Angel approached nearer, Musa ﷺ swung his fist and hit him solidly in the face, knocking out one of his eyes. Azrail ﷺ was astonished; no one had ever reacted to him in quite this fashion before. He went flying to his Lord who listened to his complaints and quickly replaced his eye. The Prophet Muhammad ﷺ said that the devil would cross to the other side of the road in order not to meet Omar ibn al-Khattab ﷺ. As shaytan was afraid of Sayyidina Omar ﷺ so the Angel of Death ﷺ was afraid of the fierce and furious Prophet Musa ﷺ. From that time until today the Angel of Death ﷺ no longer appears visibly to the one whose soul he is taking.

Now Allah spoke directly to His servant telling him that the angel was only sent to advise him that death was approaching. It was a courtesy call. Allah wanted to show Musa ﷺ the land that was promised him and his people, and also something of what was in store for them in the future. He Almighty asked Musa ﷺ to climb the tall mountain behind his encampment in order to meet with his Lord at the summit.

It was a hot summer day in the desert of Tih and the order came at noon. Musa ﷺ picked up his staff, said farewell to his wife and his children, and set out to obey the orders of his Lord. He climbed the tall, rocky peak until he neared its summit. He was not winded or tired but he was very hot and there was no shade on the upward path. There by the side of the trail he saw two men digging a grave. The pit was deep and dark. The earth was cool at that depth and the steep sides kept it in full shade. Its coolness was inviting to Sayyidina Musa ﷺ.

When the gravediggers asked him to help them he was more than agreeable. They asked him to jump down into the grave and see if it was big enough. The man for whom they were preparing it was tall and broad just like him. Musa ﷺ jumped into the pit and lay down. It was still a little short so he scooped out some of the earth and tried it again. Now it was the perfect size.

Just then Allah spoke to His trusted servant that his time to die had arrived. But Musa ﷺ was not ready to die. There was so much left to do on earth. His people needed him. He had not finished serving his Lord. He was still strong and healthy. There was so much more he could do. Allah sent down a heavenly bull and asked Musa ﷺ to put his hand on its back. Allah said to him, for each hair covered by your hand I will give you one year of life. What will happen then, asked Musa ﷺ? Then surely will come death, answered his Lord.

Musa ﷺ saw that it was inevitable. Allah Almighty led Musa ﷺ to the edge of the mountain and showed him all the land that stretched out before them. This was to be the land of the Banu Israil. He showed him their future conquests, their kingdoms, their devotion and their glory. Musa ﷺ wanted to stay longer. With a great passion he hated the idea of death. But Allah wanted death to be beloved by His friend and the world despised; so then Allah showed him their deceit and their disbelief, their destruction and their dispersal. Musa ﷺ felt saddened at the destiny of his people and he grew tired. He saw that the cycle of this world is always turning, never steady. He was ready to leave the affairs of the world in the hands of another of Allah's servants, his longtime companion, the Prophet Yusha ﷺ.

The people of the Banu Israil say that Allah Himself took the soul of His friend with a kiss. Then the angels washed him and buried him in his grave. The angels removed the shirt of health but Allah said that once taken out it could not be put back in the divine treasuries. So the angels threw the shirt into the sun from where it radiates health for all of mankind every day.

It is said that Musa ﷺ was buried in that grave on top of what is known today as Jabal Musa or Mount Nebo in the Kingdom of Jordan. This place has become sacred to all the Peoples of the Book, although none of them knows where exactly the grave is situated. Whether Musa ﷺ was actually buried there or not, this was the place where he may have spent his last moments. But there is another tradition that says, before he died, Musa ﷺ asked his Lord to bury him as close as possible to the Holy Land that he was not permitted to enter. The site of his grave was kept hidden from the people by Allah Almighty, one of His many mysteries.

Many thousands of years later, the Prophet Muhammad ﷺ, while recounting the story of Musa ﷺ to his companions, said that even as he spoke, he could see before his eyes, Musa ﷺ standing in his grave praying. The gravesite, he said, is not far from the Holy Land of Jerusalem, "by the side of the road, behind the red sand hill". If they were there he would show them. Many years after this, the mighty sultan and warrior, Salahuddin Al-Ayyubi, received directions in a dream for finding this grave. He built a small mosque and maqam over the spot. These still stand today, ten km outside of Jerusalem beside the Jordan road and it is a holy site for the Muslims and a place of yearly pilrimmage

May Allah Bless Sayyidina Musa ﷺ whose strength and majesty, obedience, and patience, remains for us a model of leadership and servanthood.

משה

47/48

48.

Conclusion

The fact that it is told so many times in The Quran is an undeniable indication of how important Allah Almighty thinks this story is for us. It serves as the basis for three great religions. Judaism is based on it. Christianity built on it. And Islam perfected and preserved it. There is something in this story that bears repeating over and over again.

It is such a seemingly shameful tale of the pettiness and ungratefulness of mankind. People have been known to use the story to criticize and even vilify a certain group of people. But obviously this story is meant for all of us - told in every tradition, in every Book. It is not just a history of the Jewish people. It is a history of the Believers. It has something important to say on many levels to whoever takes the time to meditate on its many facets.

At one level it is the story of the nafs, the self, the soul. It is the outline of the "greater Jihad", the battle of each soul with its ego. This story serves as a map to guide man through the tortuous journey of life, which is the battle with the self.

In classical Islam there are three main categories of nafs for the ordinary servant. The Commanding Self, an-Nafs al-Ammara, which, like the animal it is, propels the soul in its search for the satisfaction of its physical desires. It hungers. It thirsts. It lusts. On a completely human level, the Commanding Self encourages anger, deceit, envy, pride, gluttony, promiscuity, and cowardice: the seven deadly sins.

The second self is the Accusing Self, an-Nafs al-Lawwama. This self represents the birth of a conscience, the

Musa Kalimullah - Moses, the one with whom Allah spoke.

birth of the believer. This self sees its faults, although it can rarely curb them. It succumbs and asks forgiveness and succumbs and asks forgiveness again. This self is full of turmoil and distress and blame.

The third self is an-Nafs al-Mutma'inna, the Self at Peace. This is the soul of the one who is submitted. Whatever Allah decrees, it accepts. It rests in the knowledge of Allah's Goodness and Care. It accepts its own weaknesses and strengths without shame or pride. It shepherds its animal self and never lets it take control. Because of this, the Self at Peace is no longer tempted by desire and is safe from sin.

A normal human being does not exhibit only one of these selves. They take their turn in the heart of the believer, struggling for dominance. The heart, al-qalb, is a spinning top, a turning world. Ever on the move it is never at rest until it turns with the speed and rhythm of the universe and is at one with its Creator. Only then does its apparent spinning disappear.

Musa ﷺ and Walid, the Pharaoh, have names that bear the same meaning: son, mortal man. Musa's ﷺ struggle with Pharaoh is like the internal struggle of one soul, between the first and second nafs. Pharaoh represents the animal self, who is self-satisfying and cruel. He accepts no god higher than his self. Musa ﷺ is the higher self, trying to train the tyrant and bring him back into harmony with God. Musa ﷺ spends forty years, half his prophethood, trying to get Pharaoh in line. He is instructed by Allah to talk gently and try to entice the tyrant to accept the truth. Just as all men are born Muslim, Pharaoh was originally a good servant of his Lord; he was not created evil. Even if his destiny was written and in fact unchangeable, Musa ﷺ was shown the proper manner in which to treat all men and invite them to peace.

Many times Pharaoh almost listens. In the beginning, if it were not for the bad counsel of Haman, he was leaning towards acceptance. He loved the baby Musa ﷺ from the first. He loved his wife, Asiya ؓ the believer. He knew right from wrong. But his pride was his undoing. He declared himself God and went to his destruction, although he did testify to his belief just before he died and only Allah knows his final destination.

With the death of the tyrant, it is as if the Lower Nafs has accepted the authority of its Lord over it. It has testified to the truth, made shahada finally in the throes of death. Now the soul crosses the sea and the Banu Israil is born, the chosen of God, a believing nation: the believer is born. The Accusing Nafs is born. The self returns to the worship of idols and repents. Doubts its Lord and repents. Rejects the gifts of God and repents. Disobeys direct orders and repents. Is overly proud and repents. Over and over, back and forth, like the internal dialogue of the self. In fact almost every commandment is broken and repented of.

For forty years, it seems to go in circles; always moving but making no headway. The Promised Land is in sight but entry to it is denied. After forty years of bewilderment, finally all the old and harmful habits die off. The believers are invited into the Land they have been promised, the land of their ancestors. The soul has reached the third station of the nafs. It enters the Promised Land.

These are the spiritual guidelines for the journey of the self. We have the map, the route with many of the pitfalls, the shortcuts, the detours and dead ends. Now, hopefully, we will recognize them as we travel. As we bow to our golden calf, refuse the gifts that God gives us so abundantly, ask for what is not right for us, doubt and doubt again, we will remember the Banu Israil. Perhaps, we will be able to identify our own failings for what they are before they lead us too far in the wrong direction. Certainly we can take comfort from the knowledge that, in spite of our bewilderment, we are, God Willing, on the right path.

The stories of the prophets have been told since the dawn of humanity. They are part of our heritage. It is simply foolish to leave such time-honored tales for the movies and novels of the modern age. As Allah said to the Banu Israil when they asked for lentils and onions rather than 'manna' and 'salwa',

"Would you exchange that which is higher for that which is lower?" (2:61)

We must be like the old woman who remembered the whereabouts of the grave of Yusuf ﷺ. Every believer must listen to the stories of the ancients. We must hope to make them as much a part of our consciousness as the house and the body we live in. In that way, maybe, throughout our lives they will inform our understandings, the way we see the world, and so influence in a positive way our choices and the paths we walk.

There is a Hadith of the Prophet Muhammad ﷺ in which he warns the Muslims, "You shall follow the ways of the People of the Book (Jews and Christians) who went before you, as closely as the length of a sandal, not missing a step of the way, nor shall their way be any different than yours." A companion asked, "Shall we even worship the golden calf of the Banu Israil?" The Prophet of God ﷺ answered, "Yes."

משה

48/48

Musa, peace be upon him.

Glossary

Al-Khidr ﷺ – the Green Man – a saint and prophet, maybe associated with Ilyas.
Asher – Asher, one of the sons of Jacob and a tribe of Israil.
Ayoub ﷺ – The prophet Job.
Banu Israil – Bani Israil – The Tribes of Israel, the Israelites, the Children of Israel, the Jews.
Dan – Dan, a son of Jacob and a tribe of Israil.
Daud ﷺ – the prophet David.
Gad – Gad one of the sons of Jacob and a tribe of Israil.
Habil ﷺ – Abel, the son of the prophet Adam ﷺ.
Hadith – pl. Ahadith, the recorded words and actions of the Prophet Muhammad ﷺ.
Harun ﷺ – The prophet Aaron.
Hebrews – The Banu Israil who spoke a language also called Hebrew and who were known to the ancient Egyptians as Habiru.
Hud ﷺ – An Arabian prophet mentioned only in The Quran.
Ibn Yamin ﷺ – the prophet Benjamin son of Jacob and one of the tribes of Israil.
Ibrahim ﷺ – the prophet Abraham.
Idris ﷺ – a prophet usually identified as Enoch.
Ilyas ﷺ – the prophet Elias.
Imran ﷺ – Amran the father of Moses.
Isa ﷺ – the prophet Jesus.
Ishaq ﷺ – the prophet Isaac.
Jibrail ﷺ - Gabriel.
Kilab – Caleb.
Layka ﷺ – Leah one of the wives of Jacob.
Lavi – Levi, one of the sons of Jacob and a tribe of Israil.

Lut ﷺ – The prophet Lot.
Madina – Medina the city of the Prophet Muhammad ﷺ in Arabia.
Mariam ؑ – Miriam the sister of Moses.
Maryam ؑ – The mother of Jesus ﷺ.
Mecca – The Holy city of pilgrimage in Arabia.
Midrash – The Rabbinic interpretation of the stories of the Torah.
Mikail ﷺ – The Archangel Michael.
Mishna – part of the Talmud consisting of the written part of the oral Torah.
Moshe – Hebrew for Moses.
Muharram – The first month of the Muslim year.
Musa ﷺ – Arabic for Moses.
Naphtali – Naphtali one of the sons of Jacob and a tribe of Israil.
Naqshbandi Tariqat – the Sufi spiritual Order descending from Hz. AbuBakr as-Siddiq ؓ
Nuh ﷺ – The prophet Noah.
Omar Ibn al-Khattab ؓ - The second rightly guided Khalif of Islam, the close companion of the Prophet Muhammad ﷺ.
Qabil – Cain the son of Adam ﷺ.
Qarun – Korah in Hebrew.
The Quran – The Holy Book of the Muslims.
Quraysh – The name of the tribe of the Prophet Muhammad ﷺ controlling the city of Mecca.
Rabil – Rueben a son of Jacob and a tribe of Israil.

Rahil ﷺ – Rachel one of the wives of Jacob.
Saffura ﷺ – Zipporah or Tsipporah in Hebrew.
Salahuddin - Saladin.
Salih ﷺ - An Arabian prophet mentioned only in The Quran.
Sayyidina – 'our master' in Arabic.
Shakhar – Issachar one of the sons of Jacob and a tribe of Israil.
Shariah – Islamic Law.
shaytan – satan.
Shima'un – Simeon one of the sons of Jacob and a tribe of Israil.
Shuayb ﷺ – the prophet Jethro.
Sunnah – the practices and example of the Prophet Muhammad ﷺ.
Tabut – Ark of the Covenant.
Talmud – the Rabbinic teachings that form the basis of Jewish Law.
Tawrah – the Arabic word for Torah.
The Torah – The Holy Book of the Jews.
Yahuda – Judah a son of Jacob and a tribe of Israil.
Yahweh – Jehova – Ya Hu – I am He Who is – the spoken Name of God.
Ya'qub ﷺ - The prophet Jacob.
YHWH – the unutterable Name of the Almighty in Hebrew.
Yuchabad ﷺ – Mother of Moses.
Yunus ﷺ – The prophet Jonah.
Yusha ﷺ – The prophet Joshua.
Yusuf ﷺ – the prophet Joseph.
Zabalun – Zebulun one of the sons of Jacob and a tribe of Israil.

Bibliography

Adil, Hajjah Amina. Lore of Light. MI: Institute For Spiritual and Cultural Advancement, 2009

Adil, Hajjah Amina. Muhammad – Messenger of Islam. Washington D.C.: ISCA, 2002

Adil, Hajjah Amina. Forty Questions. Washington D.C.: ISCA, 2013.

Ali, A. Yusuf. trans. The Holy Quran. NY: Aftner Publication, 1946.

Asad, Muhammad trans. The Message of the Quran. Gibraltar: Dar al-Andalus, 1980.

Cohen, A. Everyman's Talmud. NY: Schocken Books, 1975.

Fleg, Edmond. The Life of Moses. Stephen Haden Guest trans. Pasadena CA: Hope Publishing House, 1995.

Haneef, Suzanne. A History of The Prophets of Islam. Chicago: Library of Islam, 2003

Hujwiri. The Kashf Al-Mahjub of Hujwiri. Reynold A. Nicholson trans. London: 1967.

Ibn Al'Arabi. The Bezels of Wisdom. R.W.J. Austin trans. NY: Paulist Press, 1980.
    The Meccan Revelations. M. Chodkiewicz ed. NY: Pir Press, 2005.

Ibn Kathir, Imam Abu Al-Fida Ismail. Stories of The Prophets.

Riyadh: Maktaba Dar-us-Salam, 2003.

Kotlatch, Alfred J. <u>The Jewish Book Of Why</u>. NY: Penguin Press, 2003.

Lings, Martin. <u>Muhammad His Life Based On The Earliest Sources</u>. Rochester VT: Inner Traditions International, 1983.

Nyssa, Gregory of. <u>The Life of Moses</u>. A.J. Malherbe and E. Ferguson trans. NY: Harper Collins, 2006.

Mahmud, Muhammad Bin Kanvendshah Bin. <u>The Rauzat-Us-Safa</u>. E. Rehatske trans. London: Kessinger Publishing, 2010.

Pickthall, Marmaduke trans. <u>The Meaning of The Glorious Quran</u>. London: Allen & Unwin Ltd., 1930.

<u>Saltanat.org</u>. The Official Site of Shakh Muhammad Nazim Al Haqqani Online Magazine.

Silver, Daniel Jeremy. <u>Images of Moses</u>. NY: Basic Books Inc., 1982.

<u>SufiLive.com</u>. The Media Gateway of the Naqshbandi-Haqqani Sufi Order in America.

al-Tabari, Abu Jafar Muhammad b. Jarir. <u>The History of al-Tabari vol III</u>. W.M.Brinner trans. Albany: SUNY, 1991.

al-Tha'labi, Abu Ishaq Ahmad b. Muhammad Ibrahim. <u>'Ara'is al-Majalis fi Qisas al Anbiya or Lives of The Prophets</u>. W.M.Brinner trans. Leiden: E.J.Brill, 2002.

About The Author

Karima Sperling was born in New York City in 1947. She attended The Brearley School from kindergarten through twelfth grade. She received a BA from Tufts University and worked a year at The Museum of Natural History in New York City before attending Stanford University in a combined MA, PhD program in Cultural Anthropology. She did her doctoral fieldwork among the Teda in Southern Libya - Northern Tchad.

She was the only child of an older Catholic father, who as a result of two previous divorces had left the Church, and a younger mother who had converted from Judaism to Christianity. For some reason she was raised an Episcopalian and only learned of her mother's Jewish roots at the, unrelated, deaths of both her father and grandfather when she was eleven.

In Libya, during the process known as "participant observation," she learned the Muslim prayers and fasted Ramadan. She found in Islam the unity of her various inheritances. She discovered that she could honor both her Jewish and Christian roots by being a sincere Muslim.

After two and a half years of fieldwork she returned to the US, met and married a physician who had also converted to Islam and together they raised and homeschooled two boys and three girls. Now retired and the grandparents of seven grandchildren they live most of the year in Turkish Cyprus near the home and dergah of their Naqshbandi Sheikh, Sh. Muhammad Nazim al-Haqqani.

Already the author of three children's books, Karima hopes that this attempt to relate the story of Moses ﷺ from Islamic sources, will lead whoever reads it to an appreciation of Islam and its connection to other religions. She considers this book to be a gift to her from her Sheikh, one that she wishes to share with all peace-loving, truth-seeking people wherever they may be.

About The Artist

Nabil Ibrahim was born in Giza, Egypt in 1965 but lived in Kuwait. Living out of his country he was in constant search for identity and homeland. This shaped his artistic talent.

He got his BS in Architecture from Ohio State University where he was fortunate to meet and learn from the top architects of the time who were working and lecturing there. After graduation he returned to Kuwait and worked at the Kuwait Engineering Office (KEO). There he participated in many projects including the first-prize winning design entry for developing the Sharq El-Saif neighborhood in Kuwait City, and Kuwait Coastguard. Kuwait was the closest place to home till the military invasion by Saddam Hussein in 1990.

During the invasion Nabil learned about Sheikh Nazim, the Sufi Master and Naqshbandi Guide. He escaped to Egypt, got married and began work at Dar Al-Handasa, the international design firm. In their employ he worked on many well-known projects: The West Bay Lagoon in Qatar, Taba Heights Marriott Hotel in Sinai, the Belle Ville and Gardenia residential compound in Egypt. The Zamzam Tower in Mecca was also one of the projects he participated in designing.

Meanwhile, he traveled twice a year to visit his Master in Cyprus. During that period Nabil explored the similarities and contrasts between the two-dimensional artwork of the Ottoman miniatures, Ancient Egyptian representations, and Chinese art. He fused their styles and exhibited in several galleries in Cairo. In the year 2000 he moved to Cyprus permanently to devote himself to the service of his Master. As a freelance architect he has been able to develop several projects located in both Dubai and Cyprus.

In a small Cypriot village called Lefke, amongst the Naqshbandi community assembled there, composed of people from around the globe, Nabil has finally felt mostly at home.

"Peace be upon Musa ﷺ and Harun ﷺ." (37:120)

www.ingramcontent.com/pod-product-compliance
Lightning Source LLC
Chambersburg PA
CBHW060106170426
43198CB00010B/789